BIG BROTHER

Australia's growing web of surveillance

SIMON DAVIES

SIMON & SCHUSTER

AUSTRALIA

Dedicated to the memory of
George Orwell

BIG BROTHER
First published in Australasia in 1992 by
Simon & Schuster Australia
20 Barcoo Street, East Roseville NSW 2069

A Paramount Communications Company
Sydney New York London Toronto Tokyo Singapore

National Library of Australia
Cataloguing in Publication data

Davies, Simon, 1956– .
    Big brother.

    Includes index.
    ISBN 0 7318 0292 6.

    1. Privacy, Right of. 2. Computer security. 3. Data protection. 4. Records
    — Access control. I. Title.

323.4483

Designed by Kathie Baxter Smith/Design Smiths
Cover photograph by Jonathan Chester/Extreme Images
Diagrams by Graeme Nichols
Typeset in Goudy by Asset Typesetting, Sydney
Printed in Australia by Griffin Paperbacks

CONTENTS

INTRODUCTION

There was a time, not so long ago, when I passionately believed in the strength of Australia's system of government. I had a powerful faith in our political process. And I believed that the free and open nature of our society was so resilient that it could easily withstand any form of assault.

Looking back, I can't see any logical basis for those beliefs. I was taught throughout childhood that the natural state for a society is freedom. I came to an understanding that the people ultimately have power over the government. I suppose in some strange way I equated democracy with God. Put all that raw faith together and you end up with an unquestioning belief in truth, justice and freedom.

Then one day in the autumn of 1987, this childlike faith came to an end. A friend persuaded me to attend a demonstration against a thing called the Australia Card. I was sure this would be a waste of time, and assured my friend that if the proposal was so bad, the public would reject it en masse.

All the same, I went to the demonstration. To my amazement, there were only about forty people there. I discovered that this Australia Card thing was, in fact, an identity card. It would be an internal passport. As I looked at that tiny pack of protesters, and then at the throngs of disinterested spectators in Martin Place, I understood that freedom is not a natural quality. People have to fight constantly to preserve it.

That one event reshaped my outlook on Australia. I realised in time that the introduction of new technologies had the potential to erode liberties and freedoms because those technologies changed the balance of power in our society. I went on to direct the national campaign against the Australia card, and then to work on a wide range of privacy issues throughout the world. My concerns about risks to our freedom grew as the years passed.

This book is an attempt to chronicle a chain of extraordinary events that are leading to the permanent decimation of individual rights and privacy in Australia. There is evidence to show that Australia is on the point of becoming one of the world's most advanced surveillance societies. In presenting this evidence I make no pretence at enlightened social comment. My purpose is merely to help expose a rapid and silent disintegration of our liberties.

This book describes the construction right here in Australia of one of the world's most effective social monitoring and control systems. This system involves a vast web of computer networks designed to regulate many aspects of our lives — our relationship with the government, our finances, and our dealings with the people and institutions around us.

The system is constructed primarily by government. Nevertheless, the private sector — banks, insurance companies and so on — have an important part to play in the scheme. The difference, however, is that private sector organisations tend to develop decentralised systems, which is far less threatening than the sort of massive integrated computer system which governments are establishing. Government and private sector intrusion are not yet effectively linked. This book is divided, therefore, into two sections: the first looks at government surveillance (for example, identity cards and tax file numbers); while the second part of the book concentrates mainly on privacy problems related to the non-government sector (banks, private investigators and so on).

Ultimately, however, the effect will be a merging of private and public sector computer networks. When this system is complete, the lives of every man, woman and child will be inextricably bound to it. Those who are not part of the web will be outcasts: unable to obtain welfare, operate a bank account, or move freely in society. For the rest, life will be a far simpler and more convenient business — unless the system goes wrong.

Each week that passes sees one more strand of the web completed. Every strand is woven delicately, and we are told each time that the effort is all for our benefit. True, every strand catches another tax dollar or snares another criminal. But every strand binds honest citizens more tightly to the administration of government. Slowly the strands are working closer and closer together — communicating, then touching. Your finances, purchases, employment, interests, telephone activity and even your geographical movements are losing their anonymity. Not everything will be bad, however; technology will bring wonderful possibilities. It will also bring the nightmare of total nakedness.

In the nightmare of the future, those who voice opposition to intrusive government schemes to catch criminals or increase tax revenue will automatically be suspected of having something to hide. Mass surveillance will be an accepted plank of public administration.

In the nightmare of the future, our neighbours may not simply be exhorted to act as agents of the authorities, they will be required by force of law to do so.

In the nightmare of the future, resources may well be so scarce, poverty so great, and the world's problems so enormous, that to resist government management — planetary management — will be condemned as selfishness and greed.

This is only a nightmare at the moment, but if we continue to ignore it, the nightmare will become reality. Its manifestation will have a profound and permanent effect on the lives of every Australian.

I believe the nightmare will come to fruition because its roots are already in place. We have mass surveillance through government computer matching schemes. We have legislation that forces people to report their suspicions. We have a government which frequently attacks civil libertarians on the grounds that they are working against the "public interest".

Australians — intellectually at least — are against the idea of Big Brother. That much is clear. But the conventional view imagines Big Brother as one single, towering computer buried inside a remote mountain. That idea of Big Brother, in any event, is redundant. It should perhaps be replaced by the term "Big Family". And in place of the one all-seeing computer, there will now be thousands, all linked and matched.

Data matching, which links various computers in government and the private sector, has been all but ignored by Australians. Yet the matching epidemic happening right now allows one computer to talk easily with many others, thus creating the effect of one giant computer.

Nor is the future one of a ruthless Orwellian government terrorising an unwilling populace. The future is far more likely to be the governments, the corporations and the people, working together to ensure that no-one has any secrets anymore.

The nightmare is that everyone goes along with this new order, believing the lie that it's all for the good of the community and solely designed to get the cheats who would destroy our way of life. Rights and freedoms will no longer be absolute. Instead, they will be the scraps left over after government and law enforcement have had their fill.

This scenario unfolds day by day before the eyes of every Australian. Every time you hear of another law to give someone access to your bank account; or another set of powers for the tax office; or one more obligation to give information to some agency or other, you can feel the web in action. You only have to use your imagination to see where it is taking us. Only a tiny handful of journalists, jurists and politicians are asking questions about these things, so we should wonder just who will stop these strands of surveillance being woven? The surveillance initiatives will not go away by themselves. And while the government can convince everyone that there is no grand conspiracy, the danger will continue unrecognised.

Australians have few, if any, constitutional rights to liberty and freedom. We are vulnerable to the schemes of government, and must remain cynical and vigilant. My deepest fear is that the much loved Aussie suspicion of authority and surveillance is little more than a sad myth. We have the odd foray into protest — notably the Eureka Stockade, the anti-Vietnam War demonstrations and the anti-Australia Card campaign — but by and large we accept what's dished out to us. Australians happily pioneered compulsory seat belts, random breath testing, red light cameras and even the mandatory wearing of bicycle helmets. When the New South Wales Government announced in 1991 that it was setting up a system of random surveillance cameras to photograph vehicles and send the images via satellite for processing by a law enforcement computer, there was hardly a whisper of protest. The essential problem discussed in this book is not dangerous technology, or even belligerent political masters. It is apathy.

The anti-Australia Card campaign, by this unfortunate reasoning, was an aberration — a fluke revolt that was brought about by imagery and clever management more than substance. Neither the Parliament nor the media acted in that issue to protect the public interest. The same deadly ambivalence is occurring right now with other less visible and more artfully managed surveillance schemes.

We are, by my reckoning, in the last moment of grace before Australia becomes a totally regulated society. Total regulation, total compliance and total management will bring some benefits, but the dangers may destroy what's left of the Australia we cherish.

Sadly, the law has failed to protect us from the most dangerous leakage of our liberties. Our community will need to develop radical solutions and a very deep consciousness. I hope this book can provide the framework for such an approach.

This is a difficult subject to tackle. Some of the initiatives of the emerging Surveillance State are genuinely intended for the public good. Some of the initiatives may well result in greater wealth and equity. It is, nevertheless, my firm belief that this rosy outcome is illusory. Rather than being on the verge of a golden age of liberal democracy, we are witnessing what may be the last remaining years of a truly free society. There are solutions to the crisis, but we must act without delay. There is, in my view, very little time left.

Simon Davies
Sydney, 1992

CHAPTER ONE

THE BIRTH OF A NIGHTMARE AND THE DEATH OF PRIVACY

"In Germany, the Nazis came for the communists, and I didn't speak up because I was not a communist. Then they came for the Jews, and I didn't speak up because I was not a Jew. Then they came for the trades unionists, but I didn't speak up because I was not a trades unionist. Then they came for the Catholics, but I was a Protestant, so I didn't speak up. Then they came for me ... By that time there was no-one to speak up for anyone."

Martin Niemoller, German anti-Nazi campaigner

WHAT IS PRIVACY?

There are at least a hundred wildly different definitions of privacy. Even after decades of academic interest in the subject, the world's leading experts have been unable to agree on a single definition. One pioneer in the field described privacy as "Part philosophy, some semantics, and much pure passion"[1]. At least on that point, everyone agrees.

Some countries (France, for example) see the concept of privacy as a form of "liberty". Others see privacy as being the protection of information about individuals. The popular definition is expressed in *The Macquarie Dictionary*, which explains privacy as "retirement, seclusion or secrecy".

One school of thought argues that privacy protection is one way of drawing the line at how far a government can intrude into your affairs. In that context, privacy is a question of power. Yours, the government's and the power of corporations. Privacy can be seen as a measure of how much surveillance and control can be established over our lives. Privacy is a measure of how much we should allow ourselves to become subjects of the ever-expanding

1

technological empire. It can even be a measure of how much autonomy a nation should have in the emerging international order.

A single parent, receiving a government benefit for example, might wonder just how far the government should be allowed to ask intrusive personal questions about relationships and daily activities. A clerical assistant might wonder whether an employer should have the right to monitor telephone conversations or electronic mail, or to set up closed circuit video surveillance cameras in the office. People who deal in cash for legitimate reasons might feel that the government has no right to commence a routine investigation after they bank the proceeds of a garage sale.

A hundred years ago, a brilliant American judge, Louis Brandeis, gave prominence to privacy as a concept, urging that it was the individual's "right to be left alone". Brandeis argued that privacy was the most cherished of freedoms in a democracy, and he was deeply concerned that it was not specifically protected in the United States Constitution. A century later, the Constitution still gives only limited protection for privacy.

In 1975, the Californian Supreme Court stated:

> The right of privacy is the right to be left alone. It is a fundamental and compelling interest. It protects our homes, our families, our thoughts, our emotions, our expressions, our personalities, our freedom of communion and our freedom to associate with whom we choose. It prevents government and business interests from collecting and stockpiling unnecessary information about us, and from misusing information gathered for one purpose in order to serve other purposes or embarrass us ... The proliferation of government and business records over which we have no control limits our ability to control our personal lives.[2]

One of the pioneers of privacy advocacy, Professor Alan Westin of Columbia University in New York, defined privacy as the desire of people to choose freely under what circumstances and to what extent they will expose themselves, their attitude and their behaviour to others.[3] Arnold Simmel argues "the right to privacy asserts the sacredness of the person". He believes a violation of a person's privacy is a violation of their dignity, individualism and freedom.[4]

American writer Clinton Rossiter goes a step further:

Privacy is a special kind of independence which can be understood as an attempt to secure autonomy in at least a few personal and spiritual concerns, if necessary in defiance of all the pressures of modern society ... [it] seeks to erect an unbreakable wall of dignity and reserve against the entire world. The free man is the private man, the man who still keeps some of his thoughts and judgements entirely to himself, who feels no overriding compulsion to share everything of value with others, not even with those he loves and trusts.[5]

Back in the 1970s, when academics were turning their attention to the importance of individual rights, privacy protection was seen as a key indicator of the strength of a democracy. These days, however, privacy is not a highly regarded concept. In the words of veteran privacy writer John Carroll, "Privacy was not a virtue in the greedy 1980s, nor is it a cause for concern in the needy 1990s".[6]

Part of the problem of developing a broadly accepted definition is that privacy is being portrayed more and more by governments and the corporate sector as being equivalent to selfishness or secrecy. The reality is that secrecy is one very small component of privacy. Privacy also encompasses the right to anonymity, reserve, intimacy and confidentiality. Perhaps of even greater importance these days is that privacy encompasses the right to limit intrusion and the ability to have some sort of control of and access to personal information about us.

WHY IS PRIVACY IMPORTANT?

The late twentieth century is a time when information truly is the most important international commodity. Reputation, goodwill, loyalty and a thousand other human qualities are graded and judged according to their place in our information systems. When we talk about the need for privacy, we are talking about the need to set limits on how this mountain of information is used.

Privacy means different things to different people, but for many Australians, it means setting limits on how far governments and companies can intrude into your personal life. Unfortunately, every day, the Australian people are subjected to more and more surveillance.

For a great many Australians, the most important privacy issue in recent memory was the 1987 fight against the Australia Card.

During this short but dramatic campaign, millions of people voiced their protest at the ID card proposal of the Hawke Government. So clear was the wave of defiance that the government rapidly dropped the scheme.

Unfortunately, despite the people's clear message to the government, the threat to our privacy and freedoms is greater now than ever. The technology now exists to track the movements of every citizen. Each developed country has the technical capacity to numerically code every member of its population. Every government has the ability to collect, store, cross-correlate and cross-match intimate details about people. Our financial dealings, medical concerns, employment records and a hundred other aspects of our lives are already monitored. In the Commonwealth Government alone, 187 departments and agencies hold billions of items of personal information in more than 900 categories.[7] Banks, insurance companies, state government bodies and credit agencies hold many more. The only force capable of stopping the completion of a surveillance web is the boundary that we call privacy.

If any government is allowed, piece by piece, to assemble a complete linkage of this technology, our freedoms will be largely destroyed. The alarm will not be raised until the mechanism has become indispensable.

Some of this gathering of information and the use of sophisticated storage and monitoring capacities are intended for the betterment of the community. But at what point has the individual the right to call a halt to the uses of the technology? In its quest to track down every lost dollar, does the government have an unlimited right to pry into your personal affairs? In its pursuit of crime, has the government absolute power to demand compliance?

The answer, of course, is that no government should have a limitless right to invade your individual rights and your privacy.

It is the people, of course, who must draw the line at how far the government can go. The problem is that the government tells the people next to nothing about these things. Many taxation and law enforcement schemes are planned entirely in secret. With one recent national scheme, the Law Enforcement Access Network (LEAN), bureaucrats have been instructed to make no public comment about the proposal.[8] And yet, the scheme is so dangerous that the world network of privacy experts, Privacy International, moved a formal resolution of concern at its 1992 Washington DC meeting. The government remains mute on the plans.[9]

More than 20 years ago, in delivering the 1969 Boyer Lectures, former Governor-General (then Professor) Sir Zelman Cowan warned:

> Why should we have concern for the private man? There are many who say that he has no place at all in our world. In the totalitarian states of recent days and our own day, the claim to privacy is utterly rejected. The man whose time cannot be accounted for, who has a life concealed from others, is likely to be suspected of treasonable or at least non-conforming activities. The totalitarian master assails the claim of the private man as "immoral", "anti-social", as "part of the cult of individualism". Expressed in more general terms, it is said that the individual only has meaning in a social context, so that the claim to privacy is simply an exhibition of caprice, triviality or irresponsibility.[10]

Privacy should be a vital concern for everyone, because the technology to monitor and control our lives exists right this minute, and there appears very little opposition to it. Public awareness is handicapped by the unfortunate reality that technological intrusion no longer occurs blatantly, as it did with the Australia Card. It takes place with stealth. Slick public relations consultants and word-smiths are employed to "neutralise" the language of privacy invasion. Hence the New South Wales Government's satellite road surveillance project was rapidly changed from "Scam Scan" to "Safe-T-Cam", emphasising the systems capacity to halt speeding drivers, rather than its other law enforcement possibilities (such as causing the arrest of anyone with an outstanding warrant). The English health system's Smart Card project became the "Care Card".

WHY PRIVACY IS A FUNDAMENTAL AND CRUCIAL RIGHT

Privacy is one of the most important rights of a free nation. In Australia, we take it for granted. But the importance of privacy can be seen in the nightmare scenario of a thousand science fiction thrillers. More importantly, the importance of privacy is reflected in the nightmare of countries that have none. To understand why privacy is so important, you have only to imagine life without it. People who have no rights of privacy are vulnerable to limitless intrusion by governments, corporations, or anyone else who chooses to interfere in your personal affairs. Imagine a world where government had an unfettered right to demand information from you, or to remove money from your bank account, or even to enter your home.

The tragic history of many of the world's countries shows us that a nation denied the right of privacy is invariably denied all other freedoms and rights. A nation which has no sense of privacy is easy prey for enslavement.

But why does all this matter for Australia? Surely we are immune from the threat of surveillance and control. Absolutely not. The price of our freedom is still eternal vigilance. Take a brief look at life under the old regimes in Rumania, or Russia, or East Germany, or South Africa. Their people surely once cherished freedom every bit as much as the citizens of other nations. That their rights have been so curtailed should be sobering testimony to Australia to jealously guard what freedoms we have. Part of Russia's problem in its painful transition to democracy is that its people now have no basis of understanding about principles of freedom or democracy. Hence, these concepts can easily be hijacked.

Most importantly, take a look at what is happening in Australia right now. When the government introduced the Tax File Number (TFN) as an alternative to the Australia Card, Treasurer Paul Keating stood up in Parliament and promised faithfully that it would always be strictly limited to the Tax Department.[11] Two years later, the government has extended the TFN to many, many other uses, including pensions and benefits and higher education. As recently as September 1992, the government announced extensions to the TFN, legislated without prior consultation with the Privacy Commissioner.[12]

The Federal Government has embarked on a major policy of data-matching, in which they will mass-match your files in various departments. There appears to be little or no cost benefit justification in the data-matching proposal, and a proper public debate has never occurred.[13] The government has simply assumed it has the right to do these things.

It is important to consider that when the government compares all its files on you, it is doing what police could not do unless they had secured a warrant. We are talking here of mass search without warrant.[14]

Privacy advocates believe mass matching of computer files should not be done unless careful thought has been given to the consequences. As the world becomes more information oriented, and as computers develop more of an influence in our lives, the claim by authorities for the unrestricted right to inspect our information on computer files should be weighed as a matter of the utmost gravity.

Perhaps the most important ramification of the government's activities is the damage that will be done to the relationship between the citizen and the state. As government employs more tactics to monitor the citizen, mutual mistrust and suspicion may follow.

PRIVACY ALLOWS US TO HAVE SOME CONTROL OVER OUR LIVES

There exists a "natural right" in any modern free society. The citizen has a natural right to freedom. Government has a natural right to exercise a degree of authority. But the existence of a natural right of freedom does not necessarily mean that it will prevail against the forces of tyranny or apathy. A society must constantly assess the balance between the natural right of people, and the natural right of government. The balance between these rights can be determined by the exercise of privacy protections.

The concept of privacy as a control mechanism to protect freedom is an interesting one. If, for a moment, you consider that there is a small risk that a future government may be hostile to the cause of democracy, then the surveillance web we are establishing could be extremely dangerous to the freedom of future generations. The balance between government's right and the right of the citizen can be partly judged by the risk to future freedoms and liberties.

This position is central to the privacy position. Privacy advocacy, in North America at least, is becoming more and more a matter of relationships of power. Control over the exercise of surveillance by government is a major determinant in the power relationship between the government and the citizen. Advocates believe that control should not readily be traded off, and argue passionately that a downward shift in control or protection must be avoided even where certain benefits are promised. Privacy advocates are constantly confronting the process of "function creep" whereby systems established for one purpose are extended over time to unforeseen purposes. The small gains made in privacy protection can easily be eroded, often for benefits that the public might regard as reasonable.

WHAT RIGHTS DO WE HAVE?

Australians have surprisingly few legal rights to privacy. A privacy law was passed by the Commonwealth Government in 1988, but this is extremely limited. It allows us to view and to change information about us held by Commonwealth government departments and by credit-reporting agencies (agencies that keep information about our credit rating).

The states, with the sole exception of New South Wales, have no privacy laws. Even the New South Wales law is, in effect, a paper tiger. Insurance companies, banks, state government departments and the corporate sector are not subject to privacy law.

Australia is a signatory to the Organisation for Economic Cooperation and Development (OECD) international convention on privacy, which sets out standards for the collection, storage and use of our personal information, but this is not enforceable, nor is it recognised outside the Commonwealth departments. Nor do we have any privacy protection in our Federal Constitution.

If you accept the definition of privacy as a limitation of the power of authority, even the laws we do have are relatively useless. The Commonwealth Act does not stop the government doing more or less as it pleases. Solutions to privacy invasion have traditionally been sought through protections in law. Until recently the reasoning of privacy advocates has been that if we make laws to govern what information can and cannot be collected or used, that will be sufficient. More and more advocates here and overseas, however, are now coming to the conclusion that the law in fact gives us only very limited protection. Even under the toughest privacy laws, governments are given considerable powers if they can justify the intrusions on the basis of law enforcement or the collection of public revenue. There is a real irony here. Law enforcement and the collection of public revenue are the key areas of privacy invasion. The result is that privacy law is in some respects something of a farce.[15]

THE INTERESTS THAT COMPETE WITH PRIVACY

In 1986, during a presentation in Adelaide, the then Health Minister Neal Blewett attempted to provide a definition of privacy. Blewett argued that government had a natural right to limit individual autonomy so that it could act for the good of the entire community. The view that he expressed during the meeting was that privacy "in many ways is a bourgeois right, like the right to private property …".[16] The saying was made infamous during the subsequent campaign against the ID card, when it was placed on posters and distributed throughout the country.

Blewett, however, was not alone in this philosophy. It is a view generally shared by police, taxation authorities, banks, private investigators, electricity authorities, statistical agencies, and just about anyone else who makes it their business to act in the interests of society. The view that privacy is a luxury or even a dangerous interference to efficient public administration is widespread. On my first trip to the United States in 1990 I was told gruffly by a customs agent that my business as a privacy advocate was something "that the US can do without — there's a war going on here".

One of the fundamental debates amongst privacy advocates is whether privacy is an absolute or a relative value. That is, should we agree that our privacy is a fixed and non-negotiable right, similar to the right to a fair trial, or do we agree that it is should be weighed against the demand of various interests to know our business? The answer will not be found easily. The constitution of the Australian Privacy Foundation includes the aim: "To support privacy being given appropriate weight when it is balanced against other important social and individual interests". Of course, when the ID card was a threat to Australia, the Privacy Foundation judged that there was no competing interest that could justify such an intrusion. Most organisations, however, take the view that privacy should be traded off against the broader public interest. The common understanding is that the proper organisation of society demands that each of us surrender some of our privacy for the common good. Society, it is said, needs information about our opinions, habits, finances, domestic affairs, health and so on. Without this information, government could not properly formulate public policy. The view of most government officials is that society would be far less safe, efficient or just without access to our personal affairs.

The argument makes sense, to a point, but is riddled with problems. It assumes that government is competent to use our information in a proper and relevant way. It assumes that governments will always use our information for just and fair purposes. Most important of all, it assumes that the information sought by government is always essential for the development of effective and necessary public policy. In many cases, these assumptions are incorrect.

It is true that so many intrusions by government or business have seductive justifications. Few Australians could ever argue against the need to save money or catch criminals. What we need is a guarantee that the figures used to justify such systems are genuine and well researched. Sadly, on two recent occasions when the figures were officially scrutinised, they were found to be false and misleading.

The first occasion, in 1991, involved the plan to computerise all pharmacies in Australia. The Commonwealth Government had been trying for some years to require pharmacies to use computers to verify with the Health Insurance Commission (which was responsible for the Australia Card proposal) the eligibility of anyone who was to be supplied with pharmaceuticals at a concessional rate. The government was attempting to prevent non-residents from obtaining a subsidy available only to Australian residents, but the proposal had the potential for surveillance of the whole community. Although the legislation to implement the system was passed in June (*Health Legislation (Pharmaceutical Benefits) Amendment Act 1991*), the Opposition made the scheme conditional upon the Auditor-General and the Finance Department verifying the government's estimated cost-savings. In fact, the Auditor-General showed that the estimates were patently false, and the government was forced to abandon the scheme entirely.[17] The episode shows that governments simply cannot be trusted to provide a believable justification for privacy invasion.

Then in May 1992 the government announced that its much-publicised Tax File Number system had failed dramatically to deliver the promised tax revenue that had justified its existence. The short-fall was a massive three-quarters of a billion dollars.

The financial justification behind invasive government schemes is vital if we are to weigh the advantages against the dangers. The figures, regrettably are hard to come by. A federal parliamentary committee investigating schemes to reduce fraud on the Commonwealth asked the Attorney-General's Department for the estimates relating to the LEAN system. The Committee was bluntly told that the figures could not be disclosed without the consent of Cabinet.[18]

There is a very clear argument that in an age when all of us are receiving the benefits of living in a complex community, we should not expect privacy. If we enjoy the advantages of good roads, clean water, subsidised education or government welfare, perhaps we should not expect to keep ourselves to ourselves.

This argument is acceptable only up to a point. It smacks of the discredited view that a parent has the unlimited right to do whatever it pleases to a child. A government may well be responsible for ensuring a decent standard of living for its people, but this does not provide justification for unlimited invasion of our rights and freedoms.

If all government actions could be justified solely on the basis of the desire to govern efficiently, to curb crime, and to maximise tax, we would have few, if any, rights whatever. Random searches through our homes would be permissible, as would direct government access to all bank accounts. An identity card would be justified, as would a curfew. The reason why we do not accept these impositions is that we value our right to live as free individuals in a community.

There are a great many dangers in accepting the line that a community should do precisely what it is told. We should never assume that government is the repository of all wisdom. Nor should we assume that apparently well-intentioned schemes will ultimately be for the best. A true insight into the minds of many bureaucrats and social planners gives a frightening awareness of the potential of abuse of power by those in authority and I, for one, will continue to exhaustively cross-examine the architects of schemes that invade our rights in the name of public interest.

The Australian public is requested regularly to provide anonymous information to a variety of authorities, without ever knowing how this information will be used. An increasing volume of this information is intended to denounce criminal or anti-social acts. In the United States, this has reached ridiculous extremes, with campaigns exhorting people to dob in their neighbours over environmental damage, littering, pet abuse, traffic violations, high occupancy and prostitution. Special nationwide toll-free numbers are provided for the purpose.[19]

But what is the long term effect when this voluntary denouncement becomes compulsory? What happens when cash incentives are given to provide information on violators? In the United States, as well as here in Australia, this trend has begun. Bank employees in Australia are already required under law to report suspicions, under threat of jail terms.[20] A law before the US Congress would require lawyers to do the same. Here in Australia this sort of legislation is likely to increase in scope.

Many years ago, the United States Internal Revenue Service (IRS) adopted a policy of offering small cash rewards to people who gave information about tax dodgers. The proposal ignited furious debate about the possible effect of this policy on American society. Civil libertarians felt that the cash reward offer would set citizen against citizen and effectively create a vast army of paid agents of the government.[21]

The IRS policy pales by comparison to what the Finance Department of the Australian Government is working on. The department is planning to cut a deal with informers, to pay a reward of up to 50 per cent of recovered money. The new policy is likely to apply to virtually all departments, including Tax, Social Security, Veterans' Affairs, Primary Industries, Customs, Education, Defence and Administrative Services.[22] Indeed, one of the scheme's architects says, "It's not our intention to rule out anything. The legislation will be as all-embracing as possible".[23]

The proposed legislation, which is expected to come into effect on 1 July 1993, will "encourage" relatives, friends and workmates to provide information on a confidential basis to the fraud sections of the relevant departments. A special fund will then pay a reward proportionate to the amount of money recovered. The Department of Finance admits that "disgruntled" spouses or colleagues are likely to take advantage of the offer.[24]

It does not require a suspicious mind to conclude that this informant scheme, offering reward and encouragement to anyone with a prejudice or an unsupported suspicion, is open to abuse. An even greater threat, however, in the government's proposal is that the scheme is designed to create a fundamental shift in relationships throughout the community. People will be encouraged to adopt an active policing role on behalf of the government. Instead of devoting energy to criticising and helping to shape public policy, people would be induced to enforce the status quo for financial gain.

Where do we draw the line? A civilised community must protect itself, generate wealth and foster a loyalty between the individual and society. Judging when our government has gone too far is a difficult task. Perhaps the only test of whether intrusion is acceptable is whether it can be reversed. Arrangements for anonymous denouncements such as the drug phone-in "Operation Noah", in which people are requested to report any suspicions about drug use, are likely to become permanent fixtures. There is a strong argument in favour of limiting this sort of scheme to crimes where there is direct harm against an identifiable victim. Whatever your views may be about the illegality of drug use, homosexual acts or prostitution, the institutionalisation of community policing surely requires serious debate. There is a widespread view that denouncement of acts "against society", should not be openly promoted in a free community.

The same test of permanence might also apply to general privacy concerns. It seems likely that most government surveillance schemes will be permanent components of our society. No matter how repulsive or dangerous they may become, they will evolve into integral parts of the administration of government.

In 1969 Sir Zelman Cowan argued passionately that we could no longer take privacy for granted. He urged that we spend time defining this right before it was eroded out of existence by governments. The worst fears of Cowan and others are being realised. The private man cannot exist because no-one knows what values the private man might have. Governments have successfully convinced the majority that privacy is exactly what the totalitarian states have always said it was: a threat to society.

NOTES

1. Alan F. Westin, *Privacy and Freedom*, Atheneum, New York, 1967, p. x.
2. Californian Supreme Court, *White v. Davis* (13 Cal. 3d., 757, 1975).
3. Alan F. Westin, *Privacy and Freedom*, p. 7.
4. Arnold Simmel, "Privacy", *International Encyclopaedia of the Social Sciences*, Vol. 12 1968, pp. 480, 482, 485.
5. Cited by Sir Zelman Cowan in the 1969 Boyer Lectures.
6. John M. Carroll, *Confidential Information Sources, Public and Private*

2nd edition Butterworth-Heinemann, Massachusetts, 1991.

7. Privacy Commissioner, "Personal Information Digest", 1989.
8. "7.30 Report", ABC-TV, 1991 Investigation of the LEAN computer system.
9. "Questions without notice", Senate, *Hansard*, 1 April 1992.
10. "The Private Man", 1969 Boyer Lectures, Australian Broadcasting Commission, Sydney.
11. Second Reading Speech, Taxation Laws Amendment (Tax File Numbers) Bill, *Hansard*, 1 September 1988.
12. House of Representatives, Tax Legislation Amendment Bill 1992, Second Reading Speech, 16 September 1992.
13. Various submissions of the Australian Privacy Foundation argue that proper policy processes have been circumvented in the formation of tax file number administration.
14. Professor Gary Marx of the Massachusetts Institute of Technology and others have put the case that data-matching breaches the fourth amendment of the US Constitution.
15. Privacy International, *Interim Report*, 1991.
16. *West Australian*, 10 June 1986.
17. Report of the Commonwealth Auditor-General on c.11 of the Pharmaceutical Benefits Amendment Bill, AGPS 1991.
18. House of Representatives Committee on Banking Finance and Public Administration, sub-committee inquiry into fraud on the Commonwealth. Investigation: the Law Enforcement Access Network (LEAN), 17 July 1992.
19. Wayne Madsen, *Handbook of Personal Data Protection*, Stockton Press, New York, 1992, pp. 15–16.
20. *Cash Transactions Reporting Act*, 1989.
21. Calculated at one-tenth of one per cent of recovered revenue.
22. Each department will decide the level of reward, which will be drawn from a standing appropriation within the Department of Finance.
23. Maurie Kennedy, Assistant Secretary, Department of Finance, interviewed by the author, 12 June 1992.
24. *Telegraph Mirror*, 10 June 1992.

CHAPTER TWO

LIKE FLIES IN THE WEB

"There is a zone of liberty; a zone of protection; a line that's drawn where the individual can tell the government 'Beyond this line you may not go'."

Justice Anthony Kennedy, United States Supreme Court

On the evening of 11 September 1991, viewers of New Zealand's popular TV3 television network watched in amazement as a senior bureaucrat, disguised in shadow, revealed that their government was in the final stage of secretly planning a high-tech identity (ID) card. The card would link major government departments and would have the capacity to track the financial dealings and even the geographical movements of New Zealanders. The plan was to be known as "Social Bank", and the card would be a Kiwi Card.

What followed was a memorable national crisis of confidence. Cynicism and disillusion with the government was already at perhaps its worst point ever in New Zealand history, but the smell of a conspiracy made the relationship between the beleaguered citizens and their conservative government even more uneasy. The media ran hot with the issue. Hundreds of people turned out for public meetings in Auckland, and the government began to feel the heat of mass protest.

Branding the reaction as "absolute hysteria", Prime Minister Bolger angrily denied claims that work was proceeding on such a scheme.[1] He was immediately contradicted by the Deputy Head of the Social Welfare Department, and also by former Prime Minister David Lange, who revealed that work on a smart card (a card containing a computer chip) had been going on for four years.[2]

The senior bureaucrat who started the whole affair (whose name was withheld but who was said to be the head of a major government enterprise) warned that although the government intended to introduce the card merely to establish health-benefit entitlements for low-income people, the card would later be extended to all people and for all government benefits. The card would be required to open and operate a bank account, and would ultimately be demanded by employers (those people who do not produce their card would almost certainly be required to pay the highest tax rate). Perhaps the most disquieting aspect of all was that there appeared to be absolutely no limits, safeguards or restrictions on the use of the Kiwi Card. It could be demanded by anybody (police, government officials or banks) for any purpose.

The shadowy figure on TV3 dominated the media for weeks. Public concern reached an extraordinary intensity as more and more questions were asked about the capacity of this new scheme to change the country forever. The Prime Minister's assurances seemed to have the effect of throwing fuel onto the fire. Within a week, a large and turbulent public meeting in Auckland had formed the New Zealand Privacy Foundation to fight the proposals.[3]

The foundation's first act was to distribute a provocative leaflet. In a country where the concept of privacy was still in its adolescence, the foundation tried to convince the New Zealand public that privacy was not the suspect or selfish concern that the New Zealand government had recently insinuated it to be. The right to privacy, warned the foundation, is the right to draw the line at how far a government (or anyone else) can intrude into your personal life. "The defence of privacy is the defence against surveillance and control. If we sacrifice or surrender that right, freedom has lost one of its most precious safeguards."[4]

The foundation went on to warn that a country with no constitution and no parliamentary house of review could ill afford to accept the promises of politicians — conservative parties or otherwise. "When governments in New Zealand propose any measure to monitor or control the population, New Zealanders should demand an exhaustive justification. This simply has not happened."

A great many issues were debated in the days and weeks following the revelations of the anonymous public servant, but none were more passionate than the debate about the right of government to hold so much power over the citizen. Surely the people had a right to draw the line at how far their government could go?

The Privacy Foundation worked long and hard at convincing the New Zealand public to remember that in any democratic nation, it is the government that is accountable to the people, not the other way round. Governments that argue on the basis of "nothing to hide, nothing to fear" are resorting to a flimsy and dangerous argument. No civilised population, the foundation argued, should be blackmailed into accepting a revenue measure.

Cracks began appearing in the government. National MP Grant Thomas crossed the floor of Parliament on the issue to vote against the card and later told Agence France Presse that the scheme could well "creep into every aspect of our privacy".[5]

The generally conservative print media turned its attention to the scheme. In an editorial, the *Dominion* observed "Although the Government is bent on reducing the role of the state, the switch to greater targeting of benefits means it will inevitably intrude even more on people's lives".[6] The *Sunday Star* was much more outspoken. Its editorial on the subject, "Desperate Kiwi Card push ultimate in cynical contempt", lambasted the government's lack of interest in privacy and called for the suspension of the scheme.[7]

To any Australian visiting New Zealand at that time, the situation was one of *déjà vu*. Precisely four years earlier, in 1987, Australia had fought the same campaign against the same enemies, over exactly the same issues. The Australia Card was defeated by popular revolt but New Zealanders were not sure if they had the same stamina.

In the end, New Zealanders lost their battle to bring the government to heel, and the scheme went ahead with only minor changes.

Across the Tasman, in Australia, the drama was hardly noticed. This was a great pity, because it could have provided a sobering lesson in civil rights, particularly for a country where the spread of technology is nothing short of breathtaking. Australia is now leading the world in technological surveillance. The computer databases of dozens of government agencies and commercial institutions are being linked. Restrictive laws are being passed on almost a daily basis. Government is intruding into areas of private life once considered off limits.

It is no exaggeration to warn that the extent of mass surveillance in Australia will soon rival those of the most authoritarian countries in the world. Recent developments appear to be pushing Australia into a level of surveillance which I call "Zone 5" — the highest and most restrictive of all levels of surveillance. Events during this century, in regions such as eastern and central Europe and even South Africa, demonstrate that this intensity of citizen control cannot be reversed without massive dislocation of the social order.

The government has enjoyed a more or less clear run in the establishment of this surveillance mechanism. The argument that these initiatives are being constructed to catch the cheats has silenced criticism. So, with surprising speed and ease, a multitude of law-enforcement and administrative systems are being linked.

THE FIVE ZONES OF SURVEILLANCE

Surveillance and control are difficult concepts to describe and quantify. Every society, no matter how small and how trusting, allows a degree of surveillance. Citizens in every country accept that government has at least some right to exercise control in the interests of peace and security. The question we have to explore is just how far a government should be allowed to travel down this path. There is a point where the rights of an individual citizen are more important than the right of government to exercise power.

The clearest way to illustrate the development of surveillance is with a simple five-zone chart that shows the way surveillance and control influences the life and environment of a community (see page 173).

As a society becomes larger and more complex, as its links with other nations grow, and as its technological capacity increases, it is normal for it to creep up the surveillance scale. Many developed countries have, like Australia, progressed rapidly in recent decades from Zone 2 to Zone 4 (see pages 174 and 175). Some, including our own, are pushing gradually into the fifth and final level.

Once a zone has been reached, it is rare that anything short of revolution will reverse the situation. Once a community has become anchored in a zone of surveillance, its institutions use that level as the foundation for their structure and activities.

RESTRICTED (ZONE 1) SURVEILLANCE This is the least intrusive zone of surveillance. In this rare, almost libertarian environment, government is small, free enterprise is strong and diverse, legislation is directed largely toward the protection of rights, and the principal concerns of the state are law enforcement and national security. Large databases of personal information do not exist because they are considered neither desirable nor necessary. The community generally respects rights of individuals, and is close enough to government to exert a positive influence on policy. In reality, this level is virtually unattainable because private sector organisations show the same zeal for surveillance as government.

CONDITIONAL (ZONE 2) SURVEILLANCE In this, the ideal liberal democratic environment, surveillance is generally regarded as an undesirable practice which should be exercised by the state only after adequate debate has occurred and when proper safeguards are in place. The integrity and secrecy of records is maintained within individual departments, and general linkage between agencies is not permitted. The relationship between government agencies and the public is essentially one of trust and good faith, even though agencies are aware that criminality and fraud occur regularly. The role of government agencies is essentially one of servicing the public.

ROUTINE (ZONE 3) SURVEILLANCE In this environment, mass surveillance has been established in three principal areas: law enforcement, taxation, and government benefits (which for convenience we will label the tripartite agencies). Linkage between these three sectors occurs on a case-by-case basis when suspicion or evidence of wrongdoing is suspected. However, there is a general understanding within the community that a certain amount of monitoring is a reasonable trade-off for the benefits of living in a mixed economy. Despite general support for some surveillance, there is a healthy awareness of individual and democratic rights. In this environment, relationships within the community still retain a basis of trust. In Zone 3, government bodies have assumed the role of agents of public interest.

MASS (ZONE 4) SURVEILLANCE This is a zone of enforced, interactive and punitive surveillance. Countless systems have been developed for the purpose of monitoring most, if not all, aspects of people's movement, transactions, interactions and associations. The establishment of these systems has been justified on a case-by-case basis, and most computer systems are interlinked. Everyone's files are routinely and automatically matched against each other to detect inconsistencies. Because of powerful arguments of revenue, security and law enforcement, the community complies fully (though sometimes reluctantly) with these mechanisms. There is mass obedience with little or no resistance to the initiatives or their demands. Government agencies have the role of controllers and enforcers of public policy.

TOTAL (ZONE 5) SURVEILLANCE This is the rarely attained state of total surveillance. Not only are all movements and activities monitored or controlled by authorities, but there is a complete and willing obedience from the population. The crucial element in Zone 5 surveillance is that people show an Orwellian willingness to support government control. People will voluntarily aid surveillance by surrendering their own liberty or privacy, or by forcing the surrender of their neighbours' information or liberty. The total surveillance society allows liberty of movement and freedom of association, but no right to keep anything private. The role of government and the right of individuals become one and the same. Government rights and individual rights become indistinguishable.

Until the middle of the 1970s, Australia generally exercised a limited or conditional form of surveillance (Zone 2). Although law-enforcement agencies have enjoyed relatively widespread powers, Australia's federal structure has until recently prevented a comprehensive linkage of agencies.

Social welfare departments have until recent years exercised restraint in monitoring clients. The Tax office, while it had considerable powers, tended to act in isolation, jealously protecting its rights and responsibilities. The banking and finance system was not effectively linked to the Commonwealth Government until very recently, and the mass matching of files held in various agencies has been established only in the 1980s.

From the first years of the Fraser Liberal Government in the mid- to late seventies, Australia moved out of the twilight of Zone 2 and into the third zone. The tripartite agencies progressively gained more power and influence: law-enforcement agencies came closer together, the Tax Office gained considerable power, and Social Security established rigorous monitoring procedures of clients. Throughout the late 1970s and 1980s, these agencies (including the Health Insurance Commission, the Department of Social Security, the Australian Taxation Office, federal and state police agencies and a small number of emerging bodies such as the Cash Transactions Reporting Agency) developed stronger powers and closer links, pushing Australia further into Zone 3.

From the middle of the 1980s, Australia commenced a steep increase in the use of mass-surveillance technology. Computer matching programs linked the databases of major Commonwealth Government agencies, and then in turn linked these agencies with banking and insurance companies, employers, investment bodies, superannuation funds and educational institutions. Links were also made to the electoral rolls, state registrar-general's departments, corrective services departments, the Child Support Agency, land titles records, local government, Comcare (the Commission for the Safety, Rehabilitation and Compensation of Commonwealth Employees), Telecom, Australia Post, the Australian Customs Service and the Department of Industrial Relations. The establishment of a multi-purpose Tax File Number (TFN) system created an administrative basis for much of this linkage.

While this extraordinary activity was proceeding, numerous other invasions of rights and privacy were occurring. The Tax File Number system was dramatically extended in scope. The finance industry succeeded in establishing the world's first truly national electronic money system (EFTPOS). The Credit Reference Association of Australia (CRAA) tried to establish a reporting system that would have created a comprehensive financial profile of all Australians. State governments created massive integrated intelligence and general record systems. Sophisticated vehicle-tracking systems, workplace-monitoring programs and telecommunications surveillance systems were developed and implemented. Perhaps most significantly of all, the Federal Government commenced the establishment of a major linkage (the LEAN scheme) of Commonwealth and state government records outside the direct authority of parliament or the law.

These frightening developments, all of which have taken place within the last seven years, have pushed Australia well into the fourth zone of surveillance. Once this zone has been reached, it is virtually impossible to dismantle the surveillance web. The collection of revenue will depend on these initiatives, and both sides of parliament will support their retention.

A very small number of countries have entered the fifth, or total, zone of surveillance. Singapore is the most prominent example. Not only has the government developed a ubiquitous high-technology monitoring system, but compliance within the community is virtually absolute. There exists a mass consciousness in support of such a system.

Australia is rapidly approaching the fifth zone. At this level, people will no longer question the right of government to establish surveillance and monitoring systems; these will have become a natural part of the social environment. Meek and compliant public regulators and toothless legislation will ensure that the surveillance boat is not rocked. People voicing their concern about these initiatives will be suspected of working against the public interest. Giving information anonymously to agencies, about the activities of other people will become natural for Australians. Civil liberties bodies, horrifically under-resourced, will turn their attention to peripheral issues where public support will be more readily obtained.

THE THREE ZONES OF TECHNOLOGY

The establishment of a surveillance society does not depend on technology, but the recent history of Australia and other Western nations shows that technology plays a crucial role in it. China and many eastern European countries developed many of the characteristics of a Zone 5 surveillance society without sophisticated technology, relying instead on massive numbers of bureaucrats, informers and spies to enforce state requirements. Despite a chaotic intelligence system riddled with errors, these countries lived for years in an environment of suspicion, fear and control. Technology allows the same extensive information flows without the expense or political intrusion of labour-intensive systems.

One of the most important lessons for Western countries is that our transition from Zone 4 to Zone 5 will happen because of the attitude of citizens, not because of the enforcement of government systems. Of course, any free society will revolt against the unpopular imposition of surveillance and control measures, unless the people are lulled into submission. Technology is only partly to blame; it is simply the means by which government will establish effective and powerful control mechanisms. The motivation to use these systems to their fullest extent will depend on the will and awareness of the electorate.

Technology and technological practices can be divided into three categories.

GREEN TECHNOLOGY includes all developments that help to protect rights and freedoms, strengthen democratic institutions, protect privacy, enhance the integrity and strength of relationships within the community, and improve the autonomy of the individual. Examples of such technology are encryption techniques, which create a "secret code" out of telecommunications signals and thus strengthen the privacy and security of our communications, and new forms of medical technology that reduce dependence on health institutions.

AMBER TECHNOLOGY can be generally beneficial to the community but is vulnerable to abuse or misuse. Amber technology is often established by the tripartite agencies to improve revenue systems, monitor welfare payments, or assist law enforcement. Examples include the Tax File Number system, data matching (automatic mass matching of databanks), credit-reporting systems, and the intelligent telephone network (which in the future may force subscribers to divulge large quantities of personal information). The dangers of amber technology are most evident when the systems are expanded or linked with each other.

RED TECHNOLOGY poses considerable dangers to the community. Red technology reduces individual autonomy and rights, binds people to rigorous government requirements, increases the power of institutions, replaces trust with suspicion, reverses the onus of proof (assumes that everyone is guilty until proven innocent) and creates an atmosphere of repression and control in the community. Examples of red technology include satellite-linked law-enforcement tracking systems, multi-purpose general identification cards and genetic databases.

Many of the Amber systems constructed in recent years by our governments and private organisations have progressed to the Red zone. At this point, the community should demand that exhaustive justification for their use be made, and rigorous safeguards against their misuse be put in place. This has rarely been done, and the red zone is becoming more populated with dangerous and unregulated surveillance and control systems.

THE STORM CLOUDS OF INTERNATIONAL SURVEILLANCE

One of the greatest threats to privacy is perhaps the least understood. The international arrangements for transfer and exchange of information are very powerfully entrenched and extremely widespread. Australia is an active and willing partner in the international information-exchange business and is trusted highly by other countries.

Our massive involvement in the international information and intelligence scene began in 1947 when the Central Intelligence Agency (CIA) and the National Security Agency (NSA) of the United States invited us, along with the governments of Canada, New Zealand and the United Kingdom to become partners in the Quadrapartite Agreement, which bound each party to a complex intelligence-sharing network (see page 176).

This sharing of information happens on three levels: defence signals and communications information was handed over by Australia's Defence Signals Directorate (DSD), law enforcement information was divulged by the Federal Police, while "Intel" (political and diplomatic intelligence information) was collected by the Australian Security Intelligence Organisation (ASIO).

Australia's place as a "second party" (principal partner) nation indicated that it was implicitly trusted by the Americans. The original aim of the Quadrapartite Agreement was to collect information on the activities of communist countries, so the communist-free make-up of the Australian Government ensured a good working relationship with overseas intelligence agencies.

In time, other countries joined the intelligence-sharing network as less trusted third and fourth parties, but the structure remained much the same over ensuing decades.[8]

Australia is locked into a vast array of international agreements and conventions on the sharing of information. The signing of these agreements is dependent on the advice of government departments, principally Foreign Affairs, Justice, and Attorney-General's. The only time in recent memory that the signing of such a treaty became a public issue was in 1989, when a wildcat campaign persuaded the government to abandon the signing of the Mutual Administrative Assistance in Tax Treaty, which would have seen Australia surrender personal taxation information to other countries on demand.[9]

It is also important to consider the technological issues in the international scene. Until the 1980s, exchange of information between countries was impossible on any large scale because computers could not be made to talk easily with one another. This is changing. There is now international agreement on the harmonisation of computer hardware and software, and this process (known as Open Systems Planning) will ensure that, in the future, vast quantities of computer information from virtually any source can be transferred, processed and analysed by any other computer in any other country.[10] Open Systems Planning will create a vast international computer network, reducing the isolation of nations and of information.[11]

In fact, this harmonisation of computers is already assisting the accumulation, from all parts of the world, of information that previously remained separate. The genealogical records of much of the world is being collected by the Mormon Church for storage in a vast computer in Utah. Its extraordinary memory contains information on the ancestral records of each one of us. Through hundreds of terminals this information is processed and assessed. Mormon agents have collected this personal information from the public records of governments throughout the world. Exactly how all the information is used is a closely guarded secret. The claim, however, by former American intelligence agents that the Mormon Church is being used as a recruiting base for new CIA operatives raises concern about how this sort of information is used, and the importance of keeping such systems open.[12]

THE TECHNOLOGICAL WEB

Privacy is more important than ever before because technology has raised the stakes. Computer technology is now capable of tasks and functions that astound even the technologists. As this book goes to print, the world-wide Motorola company is planning a network of 77 satellites to make possible a scheme to provide everyone with a life-long telephone communications number. You will no longer dial a telephone number: you will dial a person number — no matter where that person happens to be, anywhere on Earth.

Advances in DNA research now make it possible to easily code a person's genetic blueprint. This technology has proved so useful that many companies in the United States are using it to screen out job applicants with undesirable genetic characteristics.[13]

Plastic cards the size of credit cards have now been developed into personal computers (smart cards), with the ability to store and process large amounts of information on the details of the holder. These extraordinary devices are being introduced throughout the world, and have the capacity to manage many aspects of a person's life and business. When linked to a central computer, the possibilities for expansion and control are endless.

Advances in telecommunications technology are set to make a huge impact on the lives of every telephone consumer. Soon, Australians will be able to see the number of a telephone caller even before picking up the receiver.[14] Videophones are not far down the track, and will be commercially viable within ten years. Satellites and vehicle "bugs" can track the movement of vehicles across an entire metropolitan area. The Government of New South Wales has silently established a satellite surveillance system called "Safe-T-Cam" which will use special roadside cameras to read the number plates of all vehicles and have the data checked instantly by computers linked by satellite. Once the computer notifies that the vehicle is wanted for whatever reason, it will be intercepted by police further down the road.[15]

Simple tests conducted by the police or an employer can now determine which drug you had yesterday. Computer programs designed to improve workplace efficiency silently assess your work performance. Meanwhile, data-matching programs minutely compare your files in a variety of government departments.

Around the world, in Asia, North America, Europe and Africa, governments are moving rapidly in the same direction.[16] Huge computer systems, able to talk easily with each other, and backed by plastic identity cards, are designed primarily to increase the power and authority of governments and corporations. Privacy advocates warn that it may be only a matter of time before such proposals are universal. And as more countries adopt such massive surveillance systems, the international pressure to follow suit may become irresistible.

As you read these words, information about you is being processed by the thousands of computer databases held by governments, credit reference agencies, banks, insurance companies, the police, marketing companies and so on. Increasingly, as computers talk freely to other computers, we have to be on guard against the growing potential for abuse of our personal information. More importantly, we have to be on guard against becoming mere subjects of the new technological order.

Privacy and civil liberties advocates are concerned that individual Australians are more than ever before becoming hapless inmates of an electronic prison. Trust is being rapidly replaced by the rule of technology. The demand to obey and conform to the requirements of government is stronger now than at any time in recent history. Of greater concern is the reality that at no time in the past century has the civil rights movement been weaker.

It is tempting to believe that, at some point, our democratic system and our constitution will call a halt to the growth of the surveillance web. This raw faith is naive. Democracy and civil rights are not the robust institutions that we so often imagine. They are frighteningly fragile exceptions to a history dominated by tyranny and autocracy. The old saying "The price of freedom is eternal vigilance" has in these times become a cliché, but it deserves to have more currency now than at most other times in our history. Australians, like their American counterparts, have come to believe that freedom and democracy are natural to modern civilisation and that somehow God and the universe will ensure their survival regardless of the odds.

Unfortunately, Australians have few constitutional rights. Democracy in this country can be eroded to whatever extent the population allows. Individual rights and privacy can and are being surrendered at a frightening speed. One prominent Melbourne barrister recently remarked "There is a real risk of totalitarian government within a decade".[17] We should not be fooled by the government's expressed good intentions to catch cheats and criminals. More than sixty years ago, US judge Louis Brandeis warned "Experience teaches us to be most on our guard to protect liberty when the government's purposes are beneficent".[18]

A society without a fixed framework of individual rights can easily fall prey to encroaching surveillance. It is, however, important to remember that the establishment of surveillance and the erosion of liberty are not unusual trends. Loss of personal liberty and the growth of government power usually occur slowly, often within the most seductive of motivations. The danger is greatest when a population fails to see the emerging "big picture".

The real enemy to freedoms and liberty is not likely to be technology itself: the enemy will be apathy. Australians may have to devote considerable energy to understanding the brave new world that technology is shaping.

NOTES

1. *Sydney Morning Herald*, 14 September 1991.
2. New Zealand *Herald*, 14 September 1991.
3. The meeting was held in Auckland on Friday, 13 September 1991.
4. New Zealand Privacy Foundation pamphlet, 20 September 1991, Auckland.
5. Michael Field, Agence France Presse "New Zealand Government denies watchdog computer, ID card plans", 13 September 1991.
6. *Dominion*, 17 September 1991.
7. *Sunday Star*, 15 September 1991.
8. For more information on the Quadrapartite Agreement see James Banford, *The Puzzle Palace*, Sidgwick and Jackson, London 1982; Desmond Ball and Jeffrey Richelson, *The Ties that Bind*, Unwin Hyman, Boston 1990; and Jeffrey Richelson, *US Intelligence Community*, Ballinger, Cambridge MA 1989.
9. The campaign which galvanised public opposition to the treaty was organised by the Australian Privacy Foundation and lasted only 10 hours. It was conducted principally through the medium of talk-back radio.
10. The Australian Government passed legislation in 1991 requiring all Federal Government departments to comply with Open Systems Planning.
11. For further discussion of the impact of technology on organisations and national security, see Paula Swatman and Roger Clarke "Organisational, sectoral and international implications of Electronic

Data Interchange", paper presented at the Conference on Information Technology Assessment, the 4th IFIP TC9 (International Federation for Information Processing, Committee on the Relationship betweeen Computers and Society) World conference on Human Choice and Computers, 1990, Dublin.

12. Former National Security Agency staff member, interviewed by author, Sydney, June 1992.
13. "Nowhere to Hide", *Time*, 11 November 1991.
14. At the time of writing the introduction of this service, known in Australia as Calling Line Identification is subject to an inquiry by the telecommunications regulatory authority, AUSTEL.
15. *Telegraph Mirror*, Sydney, 16 April 1992.
16. Privacy International reported in its 1991 Interim Report that most countries in the ASEAN region either have an ID card system or are moving toward such a system.
17. Richard McGarvie, quoted in The *Australian*, 25 April 1992.
18. *Olmstead* v. *US*, 1928.

CHAPTER THREE

GOVERNMENT VERSUS THE PEOPLE

*"Liberty has never come from government; liberty has always come from
the subjects of it. The history of liberty is a history of resistance. The
history of liberty is a history of limitations of governmental power, not
the increase of it."*

Woodrow Wilson, United States President 1912-20

During the closing months of 1987, millions of Australians
participated in one of the most extraordinary campaigns in
their nation's history. The campaign was sparked by the Federal
Government's intention to introduce a national identity card. For
six remarkable weeks, the ID card dominated the media, prompting
the *Australian* newspaper to place a notice in its letters page saying
"There has never been a debate like it on the letters page; there
has never been such a cry of opposition from the nation over one
topic".[1] Thousands of people took to the streets, backing the
government into a corner through the sheer and unprecedented
force of public opinion.

The idea of a national identity card was not a new one.
Australians were given an identity card during the Second World
War. This scheme, similar to the British identity card, relied on the
imposition of rations as an incentive for registration and production
of the card, and it was dropped soon after the hostilities ended.[2]

Thirty years passed before the idea of a national identity card
was again raised. Three government reports[3] suggested that the
efficiency of the Commonwealth Government could be increased
through the use of an ID card system. Two cabinet ministers of
the Fraser Government were reported as viewing such a proposal
as politically unworkable, and the idea went no further.[4]

The Australia Card's genesis can be traced to the early 1980s,
when there was widespread concern about tax evasion and tax
avoidance. Coupled with concerns over the extent of welfare fraud,

a belief was expressed in some quarters that an identity card or national registration procedure might assist the government's administration processes. Fears about the extent of illegal immigration added fuel to these suggestions.

The identity card was then raised at the national Tax Summit in 1985 (initially by Labor MP David Simmons and later by Eric Risstrom, the chief executive of the Australian Taxpayers Association[5]), and found its way into legislation the following year. Playing on patriotism, the government called it the Australia Card (it later became widely known as the Un-Australia Card).

The Australia Card was to be carried by all Australian citizens and permanent residents (differently marked cards would be issued to temporary residents and visitors). It would contain a photograph, name, unique number, signature and period of validity, and would be used to establish the right to employment. It would be necessary for the operation of a bank account, provision of government benefits, provision of health benefits, and for immigration and passport control purposes.

The overall plan consisted of six components:

REGISTER A central register containing information about every member of the population, to be maintained by the Health Insurance Commission (HIC).

CODE A unique number would be assigned by the HIC to every member of the population.

CARD An obligatory, multi-purpose identification card would be issued by the HIC to every member of the population.

OBLIGATIONS The law would require all individuals to produce the card for a variety of reasons, and would require organisations to demand the card, apply sanctions to people who refused to do so, and to report the data to the government.

USE The number and the Australia Card register would be used by a variety of agencies and organisations as their administrative basis.

CROSS-NOTIFICATION Agencies using the system would be required to notify each other of changes to a person's details.[6]

Despite the extraordinary change that the plan was likely to create in the relationships within the Australian community, the proposal caused relatively little concern. Early opinion polls showed 70 per cent public support for the scheme.

A handful of alert journalists struggled to overcome the ambivalence of their editors. The parliamentary Opposition thought the plan was unacceptable. Most importantly, a small number of committed academics and advocates worked tirelessly to provide a critical analysis of the scheme and its dangers.

As early as July 1985, the Privacy Committee of NSW devoted a special issue of its *Privacy Bulletin* to the ID card, warning that the proposal encompassed grave dangers for liberty in Australia. The committee attempted to alert the public that this proposal was more than a mere identification procedure. It was, in fact, a tool for the centralisation of power and authority within the government.

Legal centres, civil liberties councils, academics and advocates joined the opposition to the ID card plan. Over the next two years, a strong intellectual foundation was to be laid for the massive campaign that would ultimately destroy the scheme.

In January 1986, in one of the earliest critiques of the ID card proposal, Professor Geoffrey de Q. Walker, now Dean of Law at Queensland University, observed: "One of the fundamental contrasts between free democratic societies and totalitarian systems is that the totalitarian government relies on secrecy for the regime but high surveillance and disclosure for all other groups, whereas in the civic culture of liberal democracy, the position is approximately the reverse."[7]

And, at the height of the campaign, senior lecturer in the Faculty of Law at the University of New South Wales and Australian data protection expert Graham Greenleaf, one of the pioneers of the anti-ID card push, made a chilling prediction:

Is it realistic to believe that the production of identity cards by children to adults in authority to prove their age will be "purely voluntary"? The next generation of children may be accustomed to always carrying their

*cards, to get a bus or movie concession, or to prove they are old enough
to drink, so that in adult life they will regard production of an ID card
as a routine aspect of most transactions.*[8]

As the Australia Card Bill was subjected to increasing scrutiny,
the surveillance nature of the scheme received more attention.
Greenleaf described the components of the Australia Card scheme
as "the building blocks of surveillance". The most obvious of those
building blocks were the card, the unique number, the Australia
Card Register (containing all the information and acting as an
information exchange) and the telecommunications links between
various agencies and arms of the card scheme.

Not so obvious, however, were the extensive reporting obligations
throughout the government and the community, the automatic
exchange of information throughout the government, the weakness
of the data protection, the ease of legislative expansion of the
system, and the effective encouragement of the private sector and
state governments to make use of the number. Whilst it is true
that some civil law countries (Spain, France, and so on) have an
ID card, none is as intrusive or dangerous as the one proposed
by the Australian Government. The Australia Card would have gone
much further than the mere identification purpose of ID cards in
other countries. It would have created a central information register
that would touch every aspect of a person's life.

A self-proclaimed "unholy alliance" was formed in Victoria
between such figures as the Builders Labourers Federation's Norm
Gallagher, Western Mining Corporation chief Hugh Morgan, civil
liberties leader Ron Castan and Peter Garrett, who had placed
advertisements in national publications. Several organisations also
publicly opposed the card, including the libertarian Adam Smith
Club and Centre 2000. The NSW and Victorian Councils for Civil
Liberties, the NSW branch of the Australian Computer Society,
a number of left-wing trade unions, and a Sydney group called
Australia Card Exposure. Three leading academics, Roger Clarke,
Professor Geoffrey de Q. Walker and Graham Greenleaf, provided
powerful and persuasive analysis of the government's proposals.
Unfortunately, such arguments against the card had seldom been
reported by media, who appeared to have been seduced by the
government's revenue arguments.

Future events were to show that if these people had met physically to show their opposition, things might have turned out very differently. As it was, the mere joining of their names in advertisements did not impress either the media or the government.

A Parliamentary Joint Select Committee, convened to consider the implications of the issue, raised a wide spectrum of concerns that eventually came to haunt the government. The majority of the committee, including one government member, decided against the proposal, warning that the scheme would change the nature of relationships between citizen and state, and create major privacy and civil liberties problems. The committee pointed out that the cost-benefit basis for such a scheme was speculative and rubbery, and that all common-law countries had rejected such proposals.[9] The fact that no common-law country has accepted an ID card was crucial to the whole Australia Card debate. Indeed, alarm bells rang for members of the committee when it was discovered that the senior bureaucrats responsible for the card's introduction did not know the difference between a common-law and a civil-law system. Most of us could be forgiven for failing to understand the difference, but people who claim to know what's best for the community should know better. (The system of law in civil and common law countries is markedly different. Civil law countries derive their legal system from Rome, and place great emphasis on the role of parliament in the law-making process, while common law countries derive their system from England, and place great emphasis on the role of judges in making law. The distinction was made by the parliamentary committee because the two systems developed different ways of dealing with identification procedures.)

The committee's report came to form the basis of the parliamentary Opposition's rejection of the Australia Card. Despite the committee's rejection of the proposal the government pushed ahead with the scheme. Twice the government presented the legislation to the Senate, where it did not have a majority, only to see the Bill rejected. After the second rejection by the Senate, the government used the issue as the trigger to employ its constitutional right to call an election on the ID card legislation.

As things turned out, the election campaign of July 1987 contained almost no reference to the ID card issue. In the opinion of the media, the ID card was simply not on the agenda.[10] The government was re-elected and promptly re-submitted the ID card legislation.

Until then, few Australians had taken any notice of the proposal. A rally in June 1987 in Sydney's Martin Place convened by Democrat Senator Paul McLean, had succeeded in attracting less than a hundred participants. People were privately concerned, but were reluctant to express these fears lest they be branded "friends of tax cheats" (as the government had already labelled the parliamentary Opposition).

Not until three weeks after the election did the government's good fortune came to an end. On 28 July 1987, 17 people from wildly different areas of the political spectrum met to plot the card's demise. They made a strange pack of bedfellows indeed. Communists shared sandwiches with libertarians, socialists sat comfortably alongside dry liberals, while economic rationalists reached agreement with their traditional enemies. The meeting brought together many of the country's leading figures, many of whom had never previously met each other in person.

The meeting proved that the strength of feeling in the Australian community had been sorely underestimated by both the politicians and by the media. Indeed, if Australia's media were ever to stand trial on a charge of professional negligence, the Australia Card campaign would provide rock solid evidence of their guilt. (Senator Fred Chaney went so far as to suggest that the role of the media amounted, in effect, to a suppression of debate about the ID card proposals.) In my role as convenor of the embryonic national campaign I had telephoned 19 leading community figures at random to set up this meeting, and only two had declined to participate. The mainstream media had clearly decided arbitrarily that the issue was of no public interest. By contrast, privacy advocates in the United States, for example, are able to meet with the board of the *New York Times* for briefing sessions. Privacy advocates in Australia are fortunate to get a meeting with a senior reporter of the larger newspapers.

Between 1985 and mid-1987, virtually all editorials supported the ID card. A handful of journalists did their best to educate the public, but the media organisations by and large failed to support their views.

What finally sparked the interest of the media was not so much the Australia Card issue itself, but the extraordinary diversity of the group that assembled. Barrister Tim Robertson, Secretary of the

Council of Civil Liberties and a deeply committed left-winger, found himself sitting alongside conservative medico Dr Michael Aroney and the libertarian Centre 2000's director, Nadia Weiner. Midnight Oil's Peter Garrett ended up beside the New South Wales Farmers' Association Chief Executive John White. Wherever you looked, roses were sitting amongst their ideological thorns. Sydney broadcaster Alan Jones, who hosted the event, provided the organisational focus for the group.[11]

The meeting established a trust (later to be called the Australian Privacy Foundation) and resolved to mount a campaign as a last-ditch effort to fight the card. It could be no ordinary campaign. The almost complete absence of media interest demanded a publicity stunt. So the foundation hit on the idea of launching the campaign, on 28 August 1987, in the ballroom of Sydney's plush Sebel Town House. In keeping with the strong support received thus far, the hotel donated the use of the ballroom.

The key element of the campaign launch would be its diversity of speakers. The new group finally agreed on Alan Jones, Janine Haines, America's Cup boat designer Ben Lexcen and Peter Garrett. It was just what the media needed, and the event enjoyed saturation coverage. Ben Lexcen threatened to leave Australia forever if the scheme proceeded. Peter Garrett called it "the greatest threat Australia has ever faced".[12]

Other well-known Australians rapidly joined in condemning the scheme. Former Westpac Chairman Sir Noel Foley stunned his banker colleagues with the blunt assessment that the card would pose "a serious threat to the privacy, liberty and safety of every citizen".[13] Australian Medical Association President Dr Bruce Shepherd went as far as to predict "It's going to turn Australian against Australian. But given the horrific impact the card will have on Australia, its defeat would almost be worth fighting a civil war for".[14] Alerted by the unique alliance, newspapers and talkback shows recorded a logarithmic increase in public concern.

More Australians joined the Privacy Foundation to protest against the scheme. Right-wing academic Professor Lachlan Chipman, author Frank Hardy, former Whitlam Government minister Jim McClelland, and left-wing economist Professor Ted Wheelwright all linked arms with their ideological foes to fight the plan.

Within weeks, a massive movement was under way. It was suspected that the campaign launch would trigger a turning point in public opinion, but none was prepared for the tidal wave that followed. The foundation was engulfed by enquiries from concerned Australians. The foundation's paging service, Link Telecommunications, received messages at such a rate that it had technical problems just handling the volume of calls which came through to our machine. Rallies were held almost daily. Although these were described as "education nights", in reality most were hotbeds of hostility rather than well-ordered sessions dispersing information. The strength of public feeling was never more clear than on the night of 14 September, when 3000 angry people crammed the AMOCO hall in the central New South Wales city of Orange.

Throughout the campaign, the Hawke Government constantly characterised those who opposed the card as being a noisy, ill-informed minority. The reality was that the massive wave of public rage was generated by scores of *ad hoc* local and regional committees from coast to coast. The rallies culminated in a gathering of 30,000 outside Western Australia's Parliament House organised by local civil libertarians. The Australian Privacy Foundation, which had organised the national campaign, had also planned rallies for Sydney and Melbourne which, had they taken place, would have sealed off the central business district of both cities.

The passion of those weeks approached the point of open civil disobedience; public demonstrations against the ID card began to turn nasty. Demonstrators at the Perth rally attacked Premier Brian Burke's car with rocks and attempted to overturn it with the premier still inside the vehicle.[15]

The letters pages of most newspapers reflected the strong feelings of Australians. "We won't be numbers!" was a typical letters page headline, with others such as "An alternative is the ball and chain", "Biggest con job in our history", "Overtones of Nazi Germany",[16] "A plastic tattoo nightmare",[17] "Evil and grubby", "I am not a number"[18] and "Evil weapon".[19] Cartoonists contributed to the strong feelings, with some constantly portraying Prime Minister Bob Hawke in Nazi uniform.

The Prime Minister's characterisation of the card opponents as a noisy minority seemed to be a major error of judgement. If anything was being established by the extraordinary level of community debate and concern, it was that serious questions needed answering. Nevertheless, the name calling continued, with Paul Keating describing Privacy Foundation members as "nymphomaniacs for publicity" and New South Wales Premier Barrie Unsworth describing them as friends of "rat cunning, sly sleazy tax cheats and welfare frauds".[20]

Historian Geoffrey Blainey compared the extraordinary protest to the Eureka Stockade. "The destruction of the licences at Ballarat, and the stand at Eureka Stockade was a rebellion against the erosion of personal liberty associated with the Australia Card of that era."[21]

A major national opinion poll conducted in the closing days of the campaign by the Channel Nine television network revealed a staggering 90 per cent opposition to the card. The normally staid *Australian Financial Review* produced a scathing editorial which concluded "It is simply obscene to use revenue arguments ('We can make more money out of the Australia Card') as support for authoritarian impositions rather than take the road of broadening national freedoms".[22]

Within weeks of its commencement, the campaign had galvanised Australia against the card. Despite elements of hysteria, the average Australian came to understand that the introduction of such a scheme would reduce freedoms and increase the power of authorities. Indeed, "freedom" would come to mean the freedoms granted by the card. As the *Financial Review* had eloquently observed, Australia's rights and freedoms are far more fragile than those of older counterparts. Unlike countries such as France and the United States, rights and freedoms are not guaranteed by our Constitution. A government should be committed to strengthening the few rights that we do have.

Not everyone was against the card. John Laws, writing in Sydney's *Sunday Telegraph*, accused the opposition of being "morons" and launched into a spirited attack on their integrity, morals and motivation. "This itinerant rabble is of the guerilla mentality — hit then run and hide," he wrote.[23]

The campaign intensified as news of the specifics of the ID card legislation spread. If you were in employment without an ID card, it would be an offence for your employer to pay you (penalty $20,000). If you were then forced to resign, you could not get a new job, as the law would make it an offence for an employer to hire a cardless person (penalty $20,000). Farmers without ID cards could not receive payments from marketing boards for their produce (penalty $20,000). A person without an ID card would be denied access to a pre-existing bank account, and would not be able to cash in investments, give money to or receive money from a solicitor, or receive money invested in unit, property or cash management trusts. Cardless people would not be able to buy or rent their own home or land (penalty $5000). Nor would benefits be paid to the unemployed, widows, supporting parents, the aged, the invalid or the sick, if they had no card.

If your card was destroyed for any reason that could not be proven accidental, you would face a penalty of $5000 or two years imprisonment or both. A $500 penalty would be imposed if you lost your card and failed to report the loss within 21 days. Failure to attend a compulsory conference if ordered to by the ID card agency would result in a penalty of $1000 or six months gaol. Failure to produce your ID card on demand to the Tax Office would invoke a penalty of $20,000.

In early September, a Health Insurance Commission employee contacted the Privacy Foundation to say that he possessed a large number of confidential planning documents for the Australia Card computers. After extensively studying the documents, the foundation's experts determined that the information stored on the Australia Card database would be far more voluminous than the government had let on. The vast majority of information would be "program management information" and would include sensitive personal information used to place people in classifications and categories, and departmental notes. This information would not be accessible to the card subject.

By this time, the Health Insurance Commission was well and truly public enemy number one. Talkback radio hosts had become fond of quoting a particularly unpleasant paragraph of an HIC planning document on the Australia Card:

It will be important to minimise any adverse public reaction to implementation of the system. One possibility would be to use a staged approach for implementation, whereby only less sensitive data are held in the system initially with the facility to input additional data at a later stage when public acceptance may be forthcoming more readily.[24]

The pseudo-voluntary nature of the card was becoming perfectly clear. While it was not technically compulsory for a person to obtain a card, it would have been impossible to live in society without it.

The government argued that the scheme was necessary to create a just society. A nation with such a card would ensure that tax cheats and welfare defrauders would be weeded out. Administration costs for the government would be reduced. Illegal immigrants would be caught.

These arguments made sense only to a point. The argument that illegal immigrants would be caught by the system was never satisfactorily proved. It would have been more likely that the card would have driven illegal immigrants underground, where they would have been victimised. It was also likely that the establishment of a "once and for all" identity would have introduced a lucrative black market in fraudulent cards, and entrenched illegal immigration.

The projected fraud recovery figures kept shifting. The official estimate of the cost of the Australia Card system rose on almost a monthly basis. The Department of Social Security went so far as to say the scheme was — from its perspective — of no practical use.

By mid-September, the government was facing an internal crisis. The left of the party had broken ranks to oppose the card[25] while right-wing members (particularly those in marginal seats) were expressing concern within Caucus.[26] Deputy Prime Minister Lionel Bowen urged the party to tread with caution, and suggested a re-think might be necessary.[27]

Within weeks, in the face of major protests, a party revolt and civil disobedience, the government scrapped the ID card proposal. A technical flaw in the legislation was revealed by Opposition Senator John Stone. The government, of course, had the option of re-introducing the legislation, but did not do so. Journalists reported that the government was overwhelmed with joy that the flaw had been discovered.

The Hawke Government made several key mistakes in its preparations for the Australia Card scheme. First, it had made assumptions about the right of government that simply did not match community expectations. People quite correctly felt that the government did not have a mandate to do as it pleased. Second, resorting to patriotism (calling this the Australia Card) was hotly resented. Finally, and perhaps most importantly, the government was simply not able to establish that it and its law enforcement agencies could be trusted with the mechanism. Freedoms in Australia are not basic rights. Freedom, in a legal sense, does not exist in Australia. Only government has rights. A national identity card would limit existing freedoms by imposing a state of surveillance across the country.

The government had ignored the very basic, and often un-quantifiable, fears of the people. It refused to deal with the reality that with the implementation of the card, the onus of proof in day-to-day transactions would be reversed. It refused to acknowledge people's fear that trust within society would be replaced by the demand for formal identification. The government did not understand people's concern that a shift in the balance of power would emerge in the relationships between citizen and the state. These were fears that no government assurances could ever counter. The more the government attempted to silence the fears through ridicule and characterisation, the more the fears grew.

Besides these intangible fears, several very substantial threats to privacy and data protection had been identified. These included matters of data security, function creep (in which systems develop new and unintended uses), incursions related to data matching, the improper use and disclosure of data, the inclusion of erroneous data, the establishment of central control and tracking, and the development of an "internal passport" that would be needed for every transaction and for every essential part of life. Coupled with the government's inability to establish that the system would actually tackle major problems such as the "black" or underground economy, questions about such matters aroused the scepticism of even the most conservative government supporters.

Finally, Australians felt that if they were to be subjected to a national identification system, they should have a say in its development. To be characterised as a "noisy minority" did not sit well with those who had genuine concerns about the proposal. The government's policy of trivialising the criticism was perhaps its major error.

As the Privacy Foundation pointed out throughout the campaign, no-one was opposed to genuine attempts to reduce the level of fraud in the community. But any civilised society must learn to balance the various facets of public interest involved in this exercise. If, in the quest to reduce fraud, we equally reduce our freedoms, then irreversible damage would have been done.

The key point overlooked by the government was perhaps the largest and most obvious of all. In a common-law country, who should scrutinise who? Do we elect governments to rule us or govern for us? There was a very real fear in the Australian community in 1987 that the fundamental balance of power was shifting. Justice Michael Kirby observed "If there is an identity card, then people in authority will want to put it to use ... What is at stake is nothing less than the nature of our society and the power and authority of the state over the individual".[28]

These days, as government agencies, banks, and just about everyone else tighten the screws on people to provide more identification and comply with more rules, people start to wonder whether the Australia Card might have been a good idea. Here are a few reasons why not.

1. The Australia Card would not have produced the promised revenue. The Parliamentary Select Committee on the Australia Card warned that the revenue promises were little better than "qualitative assessment" — in other words, guesswork. The Department of Finance refused to support the Health Insurance Commission's cost–benefit estimates. As time went by revenue was constantly revised downward, while the costs continued to rise. Some experts were concerned that the card would encourage the black market rather than inhibit it. This would develop when people refused to use the card, and instead used purchase and payment systems that were independent of it.

2. Fake cards would have crippled the system. Within three months of a major Australian bank bringing out a new hologram credit card, blanks of the card were being sold in Singapore for $5.[29] If the ID card was going to be the "ultimate" proof of identity, there were destined to be many thousands of perfectly safe illegal immigrants with fake cards.

3. The card would not have prevented welfare fraud. The Department of Social Security insisted that the ID card would have done little or nothing to diminish welfare fraud. In evidence to the parliamentary committee investigating the proposal, the department said that much less than 1 per cent of benefit overpayments resulted from false identity.

4. An increasing number of Australians would have become outcasts in their own country. Pensioners, homeless youth, seasonal workers, and the mentally handicapped were amongst a massive group who would have been tragically marginalised by not being willing or able to participate in the Australia Card scheme. Many would not have coped with the complex administrative procedures involved in obtaining a card, and would have been denied basic benefits and services without one.

5. The card would have created an increased incidence of civil disobedience. So divided was the Australian population over the ID card issue, that none of the campaign organisers had any doubt that the scheme would have been defeated by the administrative costs of orderly civil disobedience. Half a million people losing their card each week would have crippled the Australia Card system within a fortnight.[30]

6. It has been suggested that the card was unconstitutional. The advice of constitutional experts such as Professor Geoffrey de Q. Walker is that the Australian Government does not have the constitutional right to introduce the ID card scheme. So wide-ranging were the implications of the scheme, that state-Commonwealth relations would eventually have been severely affected. Every extension to the use of the card would be viewed by the states as having a political motivation, with the result that grave problems would emerge in the relationships between the non-government party states and the Commonwealth.

The death of the card came suddenly. On 23 September, Senator John Stone announced in parliament that the legislation contained a fatal flaw: the dates of commencement of the Bill was set by regulation, and the Opposition-dominated Senate, which controlled such things, could indefinitely delay the date. The loophole, discovered by retired public servant Ewart Smith, forced the government to withdraw the Bill. While the flaw in the drafting could have been rectified easily, it never was. This leads me to suppose that the sheer weight of public opinion ultimately prevented the government from taking the Australia Card Bill any further.

When the card was defeated, privacy advocates warned in unison that the arrogance of the government would guarantee that the fight was by no means over.[31] Indeed, the Privacy Commissioner commented in his 1991 annual report "... it is clear from the developments of the last two years that federal administration remains concerned to make the revenue savings it referred to during the Australia Card debate".

THE TAX FILE NUMBER SCHEME

Following the defeat of the Australia Card the government decided to pursue the alternative option of an enhanced Tax File Number, which would improve the existing Tax File Number system which had been used by the Tax Office since the 1930s.

The enhanced TFN was a scheme recommended by a 1986 Australia Card parliamentary inquiry, and was to be an administrative base for the Tax Office to help streamline the administration of revenue raising. The parliamentary Opposition and privacy advocates were keenly aware of the importance of strictly limiting the uses of the number. Indeed, a Senate report had warned that the scheme, if enacted, "be strictly limited in its terms ... [be] as to prevent a progressive extension of the ambit of the Bill".[32] The popular view at the time was that, if unchecked, the TFN could become a de facto ID card, or at least a national ID number.

Time after time the government promised, both inside and outside Parliament, that the TFN would be used exclusively by the Tax Office for the sole purpose of improving revenue collection. It was not to become a national identification number, nor was it to be a link between departments.

In a press release issued on 25 May 1988, Paul Keating said "The Tax Office will be the only government agency which uses the tax file number for the purpose of identifying and registering its client base ... The tax file numbering system will be administered exclusively by the Tax Office for tax purposes".

In his second reading speech for the Taxation Laws Amendment (Tax File Numbers) Bill 1988, on 1 September 1988, Paul Keating pledged "No other government or non-government agency will have access to the Tax Office file number registration system, nor will it be able to use an individual's TFN for any registration system of its own". The Opposition and the Democrats accepted these assurances, and allowed the passage of the bill.

Three years later, the government has extended the Tax File Number to the point where it is now effectively a national identification number. It is now mandatory to quote your Tax File Number if you want to receive any government benefits; to operate a bank account and receive full interest; or to work without paying the highest rate of tax. The TFN is only one or two steps short of becoming that national ID number that the government assured us it would never become.

The government's statement that "[The Tax File Number] will not establish a citizen identification system" was challenged when 1990 budget provisions demanded use of the Tax File Number by non-taxpayers. Such a scheme can be nothing other than a citizens identification system.

In a 1988 speech in Parliament, the Treasurer also pledged: "The amendments the government has agreed to accept are designed to guarantee that the tax file numbering scheme is completely voluntary".[33] Then, in December 1989, amendments to the *Social Security Act*,[34] made a mockery of that pledge by making the quotation of a TFN a prerequisite for receiving unemployment and sickness benefits.

Paul Keating went on to say: "Exchanges of information between the Tax Office and other agencies will continue to be limited to those authorised under the very strict secrecy provisions of the tax law".

Within a year, the provisions of the 1990 Budget meant that any "strictness" in the secrecy provisions of the tax law were now abandoned. The recently announced data-matching programs (see Chapter Five) will mean that the Tax Office files will be cross-matched against those of all other government agencies granting benefits, and furthermore they will throw open the TFN files to facilitate the process.

Over the next two years, the applications of the Tax File Number increased. As Roger Clarke later observed, "The parliamentary Opposition, the Privacy Commissioner, and privacy and civil liberties groups were all caught napping".[35]

NOTES

1. *Australian*, 15 September 1987.
2. James Rule, *Private Lives and Public Surveillance: Social control in the computer age*, Schocken Books, 1974.

3. Asprey, *Report of the Taxation Review Committee* AGPS, 1975; Mathews, *Report on inflation and taxation*, AGPS, 1975; Campbell, *Report on the Australian Financial Systems*, AGPS, 1975.

4. Peter Graham, "The Australia Card: A technology driven policy?" 45, unpublished M.Phil. thesis, Griffith University, Brisbane, 1990.

5. Roger Clarke, "The resistible rise of the national personal data system", *Software Law Journal*, Chicago, February 1992, p. 36.

6. *Ibid* p. 38.

7. Geoffrey de Q. Walker, "Information as Power", Policy Forum, Centre for Independent Studies, 22 January 1986.

8. *Law Society Journal*, Sydney, October 1987.

9. *Report of the Joint Select Committee on an Australia Card*, AGPS, Canberra, 1986.

10. Neither the government nor the Opposition raised the ID card as a key issue during the election campaign.

11. An account of this meeting was published in the *Sydney Morning Herald* on 5 October 1987.

12. These comments were published in an Australian Privacy Foundation booklet, entitled *Why the ID Card must be stopped NOW*.

13. *Ibid.*

14. *Ibid.*

15. *Australian*, 24 September 1987.

16. *West Australian*, 12 September 1987.

17. *Australian*, 11 September 1987.

18. *Sydney Morning Herald*, 11 September 1987.

19. *Age*, 4 September 1987.

20. *Times on Sunday*, 20 September 1987.

21. *Daily Sun*, Brisbane, 8 September 1987.

22. *Australian Financial Review*, 28 August 1987.

23. *Sunday Telegraph*, 20 September 1987.

24. Health Insurance Commission, *Planning Report of the Health Insurance Commission*, 26 February 1986.

25. *Daily Telegraph*, Sydney, 8 September 1987.

26. *Sun–Herald*, Sydney, 13 September 1987.

27. *Daily Telegraph*, Sydney, 19 September 1987.

28. In evidence to the Joint Select Committee on an Australia Card, 1986.

29. In evidence to the Senate Legal and Constitutional Affairs Committee in 1991, card systems expert Michael Walters said forged blanks of high integrity cards were now readily available for a much lower price in bulk quantities.

30. The Australian Privacy Foundation and other organisations were at the point of investigating this option when the card was dropped. See

also "Inside the anti ID card campaign", *Sydney Morning Herald*, 5 October 1987.
31. *Daily Telegraph*, Sydney, 24 September 1987.
32. Senate Standing Committee on Legal and Constitutional Affairs. *Report on Feasibility of a National ID Scheme*: The Tax File Number. AGPS, October 1988.
33. Amendments to be Moved, Taxation Laws Amendment (Tax File Numbers) Bill 1988, December 1988.
34. ss. 125A and 138A.
35. Roger Clarke, "The resistible rise of the national personal data system", *Software Law Journal*, Chicago, February 1992.

CHAPTER FOUR

THE SMART CARD

"We have to plot and plan — we must identify the enemies, and suborn them, buy them off and knock them aside to get this through ..."[1]
From a summation speech by a senior public health official at the
AHACSS Conference, 18 December 1991.

In December 1991, amidst the neat surroundings of Sydney's exclusive Sebel Town House, the Commonwealth Department of Health conducted a major three-day seminar of Australia's leading health planners to discuss the future of the Australian health-care system. The seminar — called the "Australian Health and Aged Care Systems Seminar" (AHACSS) — boasted the attendance of 48 of Australia's leading health researchers, statisticians, policy makers and planners. No representatives of the Australian Medical Association, media, privacy or consumer groups were present.

What emerged from the conference was the Health Communications Network, a proposal to computerise every doctor, hospital and health-care provider in Australia, and to link their computers. Of even greater importance was the decision in the following month to introduce "smart cards" throughout the Australian community as part of this plan. (A smart card looks something like a Medicare card, but can store considerable amounts of personal information.)

A joint federal and state steering committee was formed to take the scheme to the next stage. The proposal was then discussed and, four months later, in April 1992, was approved by the National Health Ministers Conference. The ministers agreed to endorse the formation of a business plan for the creation of the scheme, in which government and private organisations would be joint partners. A document outlining the strategy was circulated by the steering committee on a restricted basis. It advised, "We have let a thousand flowers bloom; now we must also plant and nurture an acorn".[2]

While the smart card scheme is likely to make at least some aspects of the health system more efficient, it will also be yet another step along the way to the creation of a total surveillance society in Australia.

WHAT IS THE SMART CARD?

There are various kinds of smart card, most of which contain a microchip that can store several A4 pages of data. Others embrace laser technology, and have a capacity of up to 1000 A4 pages from 2.7 megabytes of memory. The microchip card can actually independently process the data stored on it, and present it in different forms according to requirements. These cards have been proposed in various countries for health records, social welfare benefits, and financial transactions.

The smart card is, in effect, a credit-card-sized personal computer. Every time you visit a health-care practitioner, the details of your diagnosis and consultation will be placed onto your card, as well as transferred to a central computer. Thus, over time, the system will bring together in one place all your health information — administrative, hospital and medical records.

In the health sphere the smart card is known more specifically as the medical data card (MDC) or the hand-held patient record. The most significant immediate effect of this card is that it transfers material ownership of administrative and medical records to the patient (though copies of the record would be held in other locations). Such ownership might create an "open market" in the health system, allowing patients to more easily shop around for the cheapest medical services. Such a system is in place in England.

On the down side, the smart card is also likely to encourage the collection and flow of a much greater volume of patient and statistical information within the health system and to the government than currently exists. The more information that is collected about us, the greater the danger to privacy.

The smart card will rely on a new electronic linkage of all doctors and hospitals. At the moment, medical information is stored mainly on paper files, and is transferred manually from doctor to doctor, but when the government plans come to fruition, all patient details will be stored in computers. Each computer will be compatible with all other computers, allowing files to be easily transferred from one part of the health system to another. The files are held on the smart card, which is entered into the network whenever a patient makes contact with a healthcare provider. Unfortunately for privacy, the smart card information is also backed into a series of computer databases.

At the time of writing, there are between 100 and 150 smart card experiments being conducted throughout Europe, North America and Japan. Most have been established under the guidance or control of government agencies, but some have been initiated by banks. Westpac, for instance, has conducted a smart card experiment in Australia amongst its corporate customers.

In planning for a smart card, the Australian Government has a significant precedent to follow: the United States Senate is currently debating a bill that will see the introduction of a health smart card for America. Called the "Health America. Affordable Health Care for All Americans Act", or the Kennedy Bill,[3] this law is intended to streamline the administration of the US health system and to "reduce health care costs".

The smart card experiments conducted throughout the world fall into three broad areas: health care; banking and finance; and public transport and utilities. Around 40 to 50 per cent of the experiments, however, are concerned with health services.

Given the pace of research in this area, it was only a matter of time before the idea was adopted in Australia. Health bureaucrats, planners and policy makers seek constantly to create a uniform system with total compatibility. The smart card offers a chance to achieve this goal. The most common objectives expressed by governments for the health smart card revolve around efficiency, data security, improved medical service and improved capacity to generate statistics.[4]

Doctors and consumer groups, on the other hand, have a more cynical view of these noble objectives. They say the card is designed first and foremost as a cost-cutting measure, allowing the government to control the various players in the health sector. Indeed Canadian government officials openly admit that the end result of their smart card project will be "patient behaviour modification".[5]

WHAT INFORMATION IS STORED ON THE CARD?

The quantity and nature of information stored on smart cards varies widely from country to country. Although it is technically possible to do so, the vast majority of present card experiments do not merge subject areas. Thus, in Canada and England the health cards are unlikely to be used in the short term for any other purpose, while the banking smart cards in the United States and Europe are unlikely to be extended to government services.

The smart card technology proposed for Australia will allow all patient records, pharmaceutical information, and administrative data to be stored within the card itself. The existing magnetic strip cards can store only a few items of data (name, patient number, sex and card expiry date).

The medical smart card typically contains five levels of information:

Level 1. Card-holders identifying information This administrative level usually involves the full name, sex, date of birth, next of kin, expiry date of the card, and whatever administrative numbers are required. It may also contain Personal Identification Number (PIN) codes that could be used by doctors or the card holder to gain access to the information on the card.

Level 2. Information relevant to an emergency situation This is information which would be considered vitally important in the first few minutes of an emergency (blood group, drug allergies, conditions likely to cause fainting, prosthesis, vaccinations, et cetera).

Level 3. Vaccination history This level would include information on standard vaccinations (diphtheria, tetanus, measles, mumps et cetera), supplementary vaccinations (hepatitis B, rabies, influenza, etc) and vaccinations related to foreign travel (cholera, yellow fever, typhoid fever, hepatitis A, et cetera).

Level 4. Pharmaceutical information on medications Prescription drugs and over-the-counter drugs taken on a regular basis, allergies and intolerance to specific drugs. This level can be very specific, including the name of drug, quantity used, renewal schedule, date dispensed and duration of treatment.

Level 5. Medical history This more extensive level would contain:
(a) details relating to the medical history of family members, particularly about cancer, diabetes, or cardiac infarction;
(b) personal medical and surgical history;
(c) current care, with particular regard to diagnosis, current problems, treatment and investigation;
(d) preventative care; and

(e) data justifying specific follow-up procedures (this could include guidelines for the physician caring for the card holder). A significant amount of the Level 5 information concerns information relating to pregnancy, child birth, and infant development.[6]

ACCESS TO THE INFORMATION ON THE SMART CARD

Access is one of the key factors in smart card design. One of the major arguments for the implementation of the card is that more health care people accessing the smart card information where and when it is needed should lead to greater efficiency. Smart card technology allows information on the card to be seen instantaneously by many people.

One of the key Australian proponents of the smart card, Dr Rod Neame of the Hunter Area Health Service, has been quoted in the media as saying that up to 250,000 computers would be established in surgeries, hospitals, specialists' offices, pathology clinics, pharmacies and dental clinics.[7] The report of the federal/state steering committee working on this plan announced in its 1992 report that up to 500,000 screens and printers would be linked to the system.[8]

Another key advantage proposed by the planners is that access to patient information on the smart card will be controlled by the patient to a greater degree than occurs at the moment. That is, the patient will be able to deny access to certain levels of personal medical information. This, however, seems to be a fanciful theory. The overseas experience indicates that even after the usual education campaigns, few patients are aware of, or prepared to exercise, these rights.

Several of the existing smart cards have established the following access provision :

Level 1. Identification information All care providers (who may or may not include paramedical or complementary providers such as chiropractors or physiotherapists) have access to this level. Only physicians, pharmacists and the issuing organisation are permitted to make entries (place new information onto the card or make changes to the information already stored).

Level 2. Emergency information All care providers are authorised to read this level. Only physicians are authorised to make entries.

Level 3. Vaccination information All care providers with the exception of ambulance personnel are authorised to read this level, but only physicians and nurses may make entries.
Level 4. Medication information Only physicians and pharmacists are permitted to read or write in this level.
Level 5. Medical information Only physicians are permitted to read or write in this level.[9]

Care providers are equipped with a reader, microcomputer and the necessary software. Each provider is given an accreditation card to gain access to the smart cards of patients. This card defines the levels to which access is allowed. A PIN number must also be entered before the smart card can be accessed. The owner of the card may access the information but cannot change any of it.

The question of access and security are central to the promotion of smart card technology. David Chaum of Digicash, a computer research company in Amsterdam is currently working on a new generation of smart cards that will allow the owner to program the card in many different ways to release personal information in a wide variety of circumstances (for instance so that some information is released to the family doctor but barred to the employer's doctor). The only problem is whether people will accept the complexity of the system.[10]

Regardless of the idealistic notions of the designers of smart cards, the global example seems to be that there is a huge gulf between the theoretical and the practical. Some smart card experiments have collapsed because users have failed to understand the complex programs in the card. The many instructions and options are often ignored and are generally misunderstood. While it is true that procedures can be established to enhance security, few people use these mechanisms. The most obvious example of this techno-phobia might be the deposit function of the automatic teller machine, which in the early years was almost never used by bank customers.

THE AUSTRALIAN SMART CARD PLAN
The government has been silent on the development of smart card technology, and suggestions that such plans are under way have been met consistently with denials from the government.

Nevertheless, as long ago as 1990, the tender documents for the re-issue of the Medicare card foreshadowed the smart card by advising applicants that smart card capacity might be needed in the technology of the health system.

The proposal to introduce such a system has already taken firm root. A 1991 report by the National Centre for Epidemiology and Population Health indicates the scheme is virtually a *fait accompli*.

> *Patients will be able to elect to have a life-long health care record in electronic form, which will contain a summary of all relevant health care information from the date of birth until death. Included will be entries from general practitioners, specialists and consultants, radiologists, laboratories, nursing care, hospitals, physiotherapists, psychologists, occupational therapists, dental care etc. The total record will be carried by the patient on a "Health Card" the size of a plastic credit card. Copies will also be kept by the last doctor seen and by a "national back-up service" (a non-government organisation) which will maintain a network of back-up centres throughout the country).*[11]

This report also envisages the development of a new "optional" universal health number to accompany the smart card system.

The purpose of the AHACSS conference in December 1991 was to frame proposals for the National Health Ministers' Conference in April 1992. The atmosphere of the conference was upbeat and hopeful. The attitude towards information technology was extremely positive, but no serious attempt was made to evaluate the risks associated with a far more extensive use of computer technology in the health industry. Most of the participants were government or quasi-government experts, and no evaluation was made of the possibility of the system being abused by government, or whether the system might be subject to extension beyond the health system.[12]

The conference was aware of the difficulties which would be experienced in "selling" the strategy, which involves a "paradigm shift" in thinking, both to health providers (doctors, nurses, and so on) and to the general public. Indeed, one organiser remarked: "We have to plot and plan — we must identify the enemies, and suborn them, buy them off and knock them aside to get this through ..."[13]

The proponents of this scheme did not see their proposal as part of a conspiracy. On the contrary, they saw it as entirely logical that computer technology should be used for legitimate purposes within the health system. The problem in the view of privacy advocates is that people's minds become captive to the technological dream, and cannot seriously conceive that the machinery will create any problems which knob twiddling or more technology cannot solve.

The following month, news of the plans was revealed in the newsletter of the Australian Doctors' Fund (a fighting fund established by AMA President Dr Bruce Shepherd). The news sparked widespread concern amongst doctors,[14] prompting Federal Health Minister Brian Howe to say the issue was "off the agenda".[15] Two months later, the National Health Ministers' Conference gave approval for the development of the second stage of the plan.

The planning documents for the scheme are cautious about actually mentioning the smart card by name. Indeed, it is not until page 100 of the draft planning document that the words are first used. Until that point, the document concentrates on discussing the need for a radical change to the health system, and the development of integrated information technology systems. The smart card, in effect, will be the "key" that operates this huge network of computers.

BENEFITS OF THE SMART CARD

There are many instances where the lack of efficient communications causes problems or delays in the provision of health care. Many patients have experienced the annoying situation where test results have been delayed, or where medical information has sometimes taken days or even weeks to be manually transferred. In other cases, patients have to undergo identical tests for their specialist, the hospital and their local doctor. This occurs, in part, because it is quicker and easier to retest a patient than to wait for the details of tests that were made previously. Naturally enough, health-care administrators are concerned about the lack of cost-effectiveness caused by these repeated procedures.

The proposed Health Communications Network and smart card system is likely to minimise these problems. There will also be advantages to the patient in terms of the speed of health-care services and possibly even the accuracy of some diagnoses.

The benefits to the patient, however, appear to relate more than anything to the value of the card as a means of ensuring that emergency information is readily available.

Further benefits may include the possible reduction of the extent of serious drug interactions, currently responsible for around fifty to sixty hospitalisations per day Australia-wide.[16] It is equally true that the smart card will create a bonanza for health planners, epidemiologists and statisticians, because the system interacts with doctors' computers. Data can be loaded directly into the databases of statisticians.

Claims, however, that the card holder has greater control over personal information are theoretical and, in fact, almost illusory. Few patients would deny a request from a medical professional for access to information. Once information has been collected, the experience of other information systems shows that access is broadened rather than narrowed. The process of function creep will affect the smart card system as much as it affects taxation systems, credit bureaus or identity cards. And while duplication of some services and tests may also be reduced, this brings into play the issue of the extent to which the smart card may become a policing mechanism of the government. In any event, if patients are to genuinely have some control over their information, they should be able to mask such revealing data.

In a major study of medical smart card technology, Professor Yves Poullet of the Law Faculty of Namur University (Belgium) argued that the smart card technology offered some benefits:

> The advantages of the patient's MDC are primarily in the area of logic: the rapidity of treatment can be noticeably increased, particularly in cases of emergency. Furthermore, the patient benefits from a greater freedom of choice of his physician without the latter, as was formerly the case, having to open a new file. Finally, confidentiality of the data, if well organised, can be better assured, while errors of transcription can be markedly reduced.[17]

DANGERS OF THE SMART CARD

Counterbalancing these possible benefits, however, Poullet argues that certain dangers and difficulties are likely to arise. These include:
1. Medical secrecy and confidentiality may be violated because of hacking or unauthorised access.
2. Because the doctor will have the complex and possibly onerous responsibility to encode all diagnostic information on to the smart card some authorities believe this situation will lead the physician to dispense with a conscientious examination of the patient.

3. The medical information could be put to unintended and unethical purposes.

4. Discriminatory practices may arise, such as a closed network of health care where only those in possession of a card are eligible for treatment.

5. The security, reliability and technical limits of the system are impossible to establish.

6. There is a risk that medical information could be modified or destroyed, either intentionally or unintentionally.

Poullet's list of dangers tends to concentrate on the possible effect on the patient or on medical practice, but there are several broader and perhaps more important aspects that need addressing. The shift to universal adoption of medical data cards will follow the lead of Canada and Europe, where the following dangers have been uncovered by medical privacy experts.

1. The card system will vastly increase the power and scope of the government body responsible for the system (in Australia the Department of Health) and other government agencies.

2. Policy changes may be "technology driven" and will occur increasingly through the will of bureaucrats, rather than through law, or pragmatic development through the medical profession.

3. The card will undermine medical confidentiality as well as creating major privacy problems, (contrary to claims made by the smart card's proponents). This will occur because many more people and organisations will have access to a vast amount of personal medical information.

4. Practitioners will be directly liable for the maintenance and integrity of health information on the smart card.

5. Major administrative problems will arise because of lost, stolen or damaged cards (estimated at up to several hundred thousand per year).

6. Practitioners will be liable for enforcing identification procedures.

7. The programs embraced by the card system will require an increasing volume of medical information to be entered by the practitioner.

8. The smart card will be developed as a high-integrity document (one which is trusted as a primary form of identification by all

government and private agencies), and could thus be a forerunner of a universal multi-purpose identity card.

There are numerous instances where the card may create problems for patients. When the EFTPOS[18] system was first developed, the network was down 25 per cent of the day. In a similar way, the smart card system relies on a new generation of technology that, particularly in the formative years, will be anything but entirely reliable. As well, cards are likely to be lost, damaged or stolen to an extent that may significantly reduce the value of the alleged benefits of the proposal.

THE UNANSWERED QUESTIONS

The smart card plan has attracted a degree of support. The vast majority of health planners want it to be introduced. They see the smart card as the best way to harmonise and streamline health administration. Bureaucrats and politicians find the smart card attractive because it makes the health system open and uniform, and thus gives them the opportunity to make important policy changes with simplicity and ease. The idea can easily be "sold" to an unwitting public who may readily come to believe that it will give them more control in their dealings with the health sector. The media, believing these things and failing to investigate, may conclude that the card is in the public interest. So far as many interested parties are concerned, the smart card may be the simple answer everyone has been looking for.

Several major areas of concern arise from the proposal to introduce medical smart cards and related technology. The most immediate is in the technical area. The card system is likely to suffer major technical problems, and the impact of these flaws will create great difficulties for patients. The card system depends on the correct functioning of the hardware and software on the network. If any link in the chain breaks down (the card, the doctor's machinery, the communications links or the back-up systems) the whole mechanism grinds to a halt and health transactions simply cannot occur.

When Michel Venn from Quebec's *Le Devoir* newspaper went to France to interview Roland Moreno, the inventor of the smart card, he was told that the card was never intended for such complex use as health care, and was supposed to be used originally only for simple banking transactions. Moreno told Venn that purposes such as complex health data processing would create many unforeseen problems between the card holder and the government agencies involved because of technical problems with the system.[19]

There will also be human problems. Patients will respond in a variety of ways to the smart card. Some will resent or fear it. Others will exploit their new rights, constantly ordering costly and lengthy reconfigurations of the card system.

We then have to ask ourselves what sort of information may be stored on the card. Will it be exclusively health information, or will it go beyond the health sphere? We also have to ask how the information will be protected. Will this entail a series of mainframe computers. If so, how will this database be used, who can have access to it, and for what purposes?

THE SMART CARD AS A UNIVERSAL ID CARD

One very significant question looms over the method by which patient information will be backed up. Supporters of the proposal say that the back-up will occur in two locations. One is the computer of the last doctor seen by the patient. The second is a decentralised database run by a private company. In the modern context, the term "decentralised" is irrelevant. The effect of several databases in different parts of the country all communicating with one another will be effectively the same as one central database. The emergence of such a repository of personal medical information raises a great many concerns. Among the most dangerous are the vulnerability of such a database to attacks from computer hackers, the accidental or intentional destruction of the database, and the potential of mass surveillance of the population's medical records by government and law enforcement agencies.

We must also be vitally concerned about possible future purposes of the card. What guarantees will exist that the smart card will not be used for non-medical purposes? Will the central database be isolated from government use? With the emergence of genetic coding and identification, is there any risk that smart cards will be used as a vehicle for the storage of DNA information (17 states in the United States have now passed legislation allowing government to collect DNA codes)? Once DNA codes are stored in a smart card, there would exist opportunities to classify people according to genetic characteristics — many of which may not yet have appeared.

In 1991, during the controversy in New Zealand over the suggestion that smart cards should be introduced for government benefits, one private company reminded a nervous television audience that the technology existed to encode a fingerprint into the card.[20] Australian banks are already issuing fingerprint encoded smart cards to staff who need to gain access to the inside of Automatic Teller Machines. Without care, this may become a precedent for finger printing anyone dealing with money.

The smart card issues go well beyond the health-care sector. Micro Card Technologies, a computer research company based in the United States, is proposing the use of smart cards that contain criminal histories, digital face image, fingerprints, medical histories, insurance information, driver's licence, and driving history.[21] Right at the moment, such interlinking of functions is in its infancy, and most attempts to "educate" the public in the use of such complex card functions has failed. The development, however, of more user-friendly cards is likely to change this resistance.

The temptation to introduce these cards may be irresistible. Smart cards that house the genetic or biological details (known in the trade as biometric technology) of the holder would go a long way to eliminating fraud, because they would demand biological identification before each bank or government transaction. A US company, Comparator Systems Corporation, has developed such a card, which will be manufactured in Malaysia for world-wide distribution in 1993. The card, designed for multiple uses, potentially links all government and private sector information.[22]

The extension of use of the health smart card would be made far easier if it was generally carried at all times by the population. Overseas health authorities have tended to avoid the issue of whether the health smart card should be carried at all times, but the existence of emergency medical information on the second access level of the card rather indicates that there is an expectation that it should be kept permanently in the wallet or purse. A briefing document for Quebec's Project Carte Santé subtly suggests "The credit card size of the Health Card is designed to enable the holder to carry it at all times".

During the planning for the Australia Card, the Health Insurance Commission dreamed up the priceless expression "pseudo-voluntariness" to describe the ultimate status of their proposed card. Certainly if the card is of a high enough integrity (if it can be trusted to be highly accurate, perhaps with an encoded fingerprint or access codes), it would be a valuable document indeed for a range of other purposes. The Australia Card controversy is likely to put governments off the idea of forcing people to carry a smart card, or even to obtain one. The most likely scenario, however, is that failure to obtain a smart card will result, as with the failure to obtain a Tax File Number, in loss of health-care benefits and a requirement to pay the full cost of medical services.

Professor Yves Poullet warns that one problem of having a smart card which is constantly carried around by the patient is that larger volumes of information can be added to it through increasing numbers of access points. Once people have become accustomed to the enhanced spectrum of information on the card, a multitude of people can have access to it. Its evolution into a national ID card could follow.

The smart card can be used for a virtually limitless spectrum of purposes. Experiments are under way in a dozen fields and for a hundred or more distinct applications. One national newspaper warned "A troublesome teenager might be placed under curfew by programming his or her movements on public transport; a habitual drink driver could be prevented from buying alcohol."[23]

Citing US privacy expert Professor James Rule, the article continued, "A technology or database developed for a specific use may find itself serving purposes its architects never anticipated; this illustrates the need to anticipate, rather than react to, threats to privacy.

"In the future, government welfare agencies, determined that their handouts will be used for the social purpose intended, could make payments into the recipients' smart cards, which were programmed to force changes in spending habits. And the agencies would be able to police spending because many supermarkets already itemise their goods by scanning bar codes".

Speaking in Sydney in 1989, Rule warned that the creators and controllers of such systems had a great deal of trust placed in them. Advocacy groups such as the Australian Privacy Foundation and Privacy International have consistently warned that the utmost public vigilance is required to ensure that these systems do not develop new and uninvited roles.

On 15 September 1992, Deputy Prime Minister Brian Howe issued a news release stating that the government was not engaged in the development of a smart card. Five days later, however, the Australian Doctors' Fund released details of a July 1992 Draft National Standard for Smart Cards. Two federal government departments and all state governments were represented on the committee responsible for the draft.[24]

NOTES

1. Remarks reported by Dr Bruce Shepherd in *Australian Doctor Weekly*, 7 February 1992, Sydney.
2. "The Compelling Case", Joint federal/state Steering Committee for Health Information Management and Technology, February 1992.
3. (Bill S.1227 of the 1st session) amends the *Public Health Service Act*, the *Social Security Act*, and the Internal Revenue Code of 1986.
4. *Project Carte Santé*, 1992.
5. Canadian Health authorities interview with author, Montreal, February 1992.
6. *Project Carte Santé*, 1992.
7. *Telegraph Mirror*, Sydney, 5 December 1991.
8. "The Compelling Case", Joint federal/state Steering Committee for Health Information Management and Technology, February 1992.
9. *Project Carte Santé*, 1992.
10. D. Chaum interview with author, Amsterdam, February 1992.
11. Walker *et al*, *Health Information Issues in General Practice in Australia*, National Centre for Epidemiology and Population Health, Discussion Paper No. 2, ANU, Canberra 1991.
12. See "The Technological Web", a report by the author to the Australian Doctors' Fund, 1992.
13. See note 1.
14. The Australian Doctors' Fund lobbied heavily against the scheme, and distributed a report which highlighted dangers of the smart card proposal.
15. *Telegraph*, Brisbane, February 1992.
16. *Telegraph Mirror*, Sydney, 5 December 1991.
17. Poullet, Yves, "The medical Data Card — data protection issues," in *Computer Law and Security Report*, UK, Sept/Oct, Nov/Dec 1990, Jan/Feb 1991.

18. Acronym for Electronic Funds Transfer at Point of Sale, a national payments system allowing consumers to pay for purchases using debit cards.
19. M. Venn interview with author, Montreal, February 1992.
20. TV1, 13 September 1991.
21. Presented at the Third National Court Technology Conference, Dallas, Texas, 1991.
22. *Australian Financial Review*, 15 May 1989.
23. *Australian*, 23 June 1992.
24. "Patient-held medical records cards", Standards Australia, Draft National Standard 92124, 15 July 1992.

....

CHAPTER FIVE

THE COMPUTER-MATCHING EPIDEMIC

"The true danger is when liberty is nibbled away, for expedience, and by parts."

Edmund Burke

Australians are now becoming used to the idea of being numbered, by Tax File Numbers, social security numbers, Medicare numbers, passport numbers, driver's licence numbers, higher education scheme student numbers, all the way to bank account numbers, credit card numbers and insurance claim numbers. The proposed National Health Communications Network will create yet another numbering system.

Each number represents a huge personal identification system and each system is controlled by a vast computer network. Each computer network serves a particular function in society.

Many people accept this state of affairs quite happily. Indeed one of the safeguards of privacy is the sheer variety of different numbers we use in our day-to-day life. While many different systems work independently on their individual tasks, the risk of establishing a Big Brother society is minimised. While we have twenty different credit, identification and authorisation cards in our wallets, there is at least a reasonable probability that not all of them are going to malfunction at once. If, for whatever reason, we have a problem with one organisation, and have our card cancelled, we are unlikely to suffer a domino effect in all the other organisations with which we have a relationship.

In a vast and complex society, these systems can be justified on the basis that they improve efficiency and help organisations to provide a better service to the community. Therefore, despite all the problems that such computerisation may create, a society will probably come down in the end on the side of technology.

But what happens if you start to link these computers? What if you decide that the computer that runs Social Security should be linked to the one running Veterans' Affairs? What if you then link these to the Tax Office, and then to the police? What if you decide that in the quest for efficiency and effective law enforcement, all computers throughout the nation should be joined?

This process has already begun (see page 177). It is known quite simply as computer matching.

WHAT IS COMPUTER MATCHING?

Computer matching (also known as parallel matching, bulk matching, record linkage, mass matching, cross matching, joint running or data matching) is the process of automatically comparing and analysing records of a person from two or more sources. Thus, the records of the Department of Social Security (DSS) can be matched against the records of the Australian Tax Office, or the records of the Department of Veteran's Affairs can be matched against the Department of Immigration, Local Government and Ethnic Affairs. The government is able to identify discrepancies between the files.

Most government departments are now moving to some form of data-matching program. In 1991, more than 30 major programs were in progress. The number of times that files are matched against each other in some of the key programs is quite staggering. Creators of the new DSS program envisage that there will be as many as 375–750 trillion (375–750,000,000,000,000) attempted file matches per annum.[1]

The genesis of computer matching goes back to 1977, to a time when the United States' bureaucracy was just glimpsing the possibilities of computerisation. The Department of Health, Education and Welfare (now the Department of Health and Human Services), decided to match all its computer welfare records automatically against the employee files of Federal Government departments. It was a massive undertaking with the aim of exposing welfare fraud, and was heralded as a milestone in law enforcement. The ambitious plan was to allow these new-fangled computers to conduct the searches themselves, rapidly and accurately matching the data on one set of files with the data on another. If a person had conflicting information in different agencies, the computer would detect this. Simple and logical.

Project Match, as it was known, came up with 33,000 "raw hits"

— instances where the information on a person's welfare file did not square with the employment file (indicating that the person was working and receiving benefits at the same time).

The office celebrations were toned down a touch when it was discovered that the majority of these hits were not valid. Still, 7100 cases remained. Sadly for the participating departments, much of the information that led to the matches was either false or irrelevant, and only 638 cases ended up being referred for internal investigation.

Of the 638 investigations, only 55 resulted in prosecutions, and of these, a mere 35 minor convictions were secured. No conviction resulted in a jail term, and less than $10,000 in fines were levied.[2]

No-one will ever know the extent of the distress and humiliation this exercise caused to tens of thousands of honest people, but, ironically, while the results of this multi-million dollar exercise was so obviously a failure, the relevant departments hailed it as a great success. This deception has always been a feature of efforts to match computer records, not just in the United States but in all countries.

COMPUTER MATCHING IN AUSTRALIA

No-one has ever been able to calculate the extent of fraud in Australia. Estimates of fraud on the Commonwealth vary from three billion dollars per annum, to as high as twenty-five billion dollars. Rorts in welfare and on the Tax Office are regularly discovered and government is generally riddled with inefficiencies. Fraud investigation is hampered by human and technical problems, so getting computers to talk freely to each other might solve some of these age-old problems.

Indeed, any effort to harmonise the administrative systems within government are certain to uncover a degree of fraud. Some government departments also reason that the process of matching the computers in different departments has a deterrent effect in combating fraud (if people think they are likely to be caught, they won't attempt to commit fraud in the first place).

One of the principal arguments used by departments to justify computer matching is that not to do so will result in loss of revenue to the government. It is, in many ways, a difficult argument to oppose. Times are tough. Every dollar lost to fraud is a dollar that could have helped a single mother or a struggling primary school. Computer matching does not raise the ire of the community because it is silent and invisible. It is also difficult to raise an objection to it because people have come to believe that information held by government agencies is the property of the government. By this reasoning it is often felt that it is the right of the government to do with the information whatever it wishes.

THE LEAN SCHEME

Australia's complex political and administrative system has created problems over many years for fraud investigation. Commonwealth agencies have routinely consulted state records (most of which contain publicly available information such as land titles), but the work has been cumbersome and expensive. In an effort to streamline the process of investigation, the Attorney-General's Department has developed a scheme that will establish a computer link between many state and federal agencies.

The plan arose from a 1987 report into fraud against the Commonwealth, which urged states to join with the Commonwealth in computerising and matching records.

The purpose of the new system is to assist law enforcement and revenue protection for the Commonwealth. It will provide access to data, 24 hours a day, seven days a week, for law enforcement and revenue collection purposes. The scheme will initially include:
• land title data (from all states and territories);
• Corporate Affairs data; and
• other publicly available data related to corporate and land records.

The following agencies will have access to the information:
• Australian Bureau of Criminal Intelligence (ABCI)
• Australian Customs Service (ACS)
• Commonwealth Attorney-General's Department (A-G's)
• Australian Federal Police (AFP)
• Australian Tax Office (ATO)
• Department of Employment, Education and Training (DEET)
• Department of Defence (Defence)
• Office of Commonwealth Director of Public Prosecutions (DPP)
• National Crime Authority (NCA)

Numerous other state and federal agencies have expressed a desire to link with the system. Among them are the Department of Finance, the Australian Securities Commission, the Cash Transactions Reports Agency, the Department of Immigration, local Government and Ethnic Affairs, the Department of Administrative Services and the Health Insurance Commission. It is quite possible that the Department of Social Security will join at a future date. It is even more likely that the state registries of births, deaths and marriages will also join.

The system will be able to:
- search, collate and analyse the data;
- match files;
- annotate, sort, collate, index, cross-reference, link, and extract relevant data into separate files;
- prepare documents;
- conduct financial analyses; and
- prepare charts of organisational and individual inter-relationships, schedules of documents and chronologies of events

The databases will be updated daily.

In mid-1991, the government envisaged 500 terminals would be immediately connected to the system, with a total projected figure of 3000 terminals. By the time the tender documents were released in late 1991, this figure had risen sharply to an initial connection of 6484 terminals, rising to 10,254 terminals.

According to current plans the terminals will be distributed as follows:

Agency	Initial number of terminals	Projected number of terminals	Total terminals throughout department
ABCI	30	30	100
ACS	300	300	1,500
A-G's	50	50	2,000
AFP	12	50	unknown
ATO	6,000	9,000	6,000–13,000
DEET	12	24	unknown
Defence	50	800	unknown
DPP	20	20	400–600
NCA	10	10	unknown
TOTAL	6,484	10,254	

The system is expected to grow further as states request access for their own law-enforcement purposes, and as other Commonwealth agencies such as the Health Insurance Commission or the Department of Social Security join the system.

The uses of LEAN are virtually limitless. The Australian Tax Office informed the 1992 Sub-Committee on Fraud on the Commonwealth, "We were going to use it for a number of activities. One was the capital gains issue. We were going to use it for tracing defaulting taxpayers. We were going to use it for identification of rental income that is undisclosed. There is a lot of use that we can make of the LEAN system."

In the same hearing, the Defence Department suggested that savings could be made through LEAN by "tightening up eligibility criteria in the personal entitlements area, both of civilians and of servicemen: housing, travel, living away from home and things like that".

Meanwhile, the police would use the system to track possible uses of defrauded money (land purchases, and so on), while Social Security would use it to ensure that clients were telling the truth about their assets.

It is proposed that the system will be installed and implemented by June 1993.

Despite the very clear commitment made by the government to confidentiality and data security, there are numerous grave privacy and individual rights concerns that arise from the development of the LEAN scheme.

1. There is little justification for associating law-abiding members of the community with a criminal investigation system, nor is there adequate justification for prior suspicion of guilt.

2. In the view of privacy advocates, there is a very clear breach of the spirit of the Privacy Act. Information given for one purpose (for example, for land records) is being used for another entirely different purpose.

3. It appears the LEAN system will not be governed by an Act of parliament, and thus there is likely to be only very limited legal authority or parliamentary scrutiny of the scheme.[3]

4. The information will be available to a large number of public service staff with limited investigative training.[4]

5. There is a very grave risk that the scheme will suffer function

creep by being merged with information sources that are not publicly available, and by developing a wider range of purposes for state and commonwealth departments.

6. No consultation has yet been undertaken with public interest, advocacy groups or the general public.

COMPUTER MATCHING — THE VIEW OF PRIVACY ADVOCATES

At first glimpse, the idea of automatically matching one set of computer records with another seems to be fairly innocuous. Surely no-one could object to the government checking its files to weed out the cheats? The reality is far more complex.

Data matching is the technological equivalent of a general warrant on the entire population. It is no different to the notion of police being empowered to enter your home in your absence, search through your papers, and take what copies they wish.

Such a comparison might at first sound extreme, but it is an accurate parallel, and will become more obvious in future years as a greater amount of information about us is stored on computer. In 1986, the United States Office of Technology Assessment concluded "Computer matches are inherently mass or class investigations".

Despite the possibility of computer matching yielding revenue for the government, there are several fundamental problems with the process. The first and perhaps most important is whether a government has a right to place a population under this form of surveillance (known amongst privacy advocates as dataveillance). Civil libertarians argue that even if savings are possible, we should not lose sight of the principal that no government has an absolute right to do as it pleases with our personal details. Data matching is directly equivalent to arbitrary investigation without cause of suspicion.

Within this broad concern, there are three distinct human rights and privacy dilemmas. First, data matching is based on an assumption of guilt. Each member of the population, according to the rationale of the data-matching programs, is a suspect and therefore a potential criminal. The presumption of innocence no longer exists. A computer-matching program therefore reverses the entire basis of the judicial system.

In 1992, the Privacy Commissioner warned:

Pro-active gathering of information, while evidently a common element in fraud control activity, tends to be broad in scope. If it is not strictly limited and linked to a well-defined purpose, it is liable to become a mechanism for the broad, routine monitoring of individuals' activities ... the justification for more speculative intelligence gathering is likely to be more complex, and the definition of what information is relevant or necessary more vague. It is important that clear boundaries be established for information gathering in the pro-active detection of fraud ... It is inherent in the design of data-matching programs that they are not able to justify individually each disclosure of information involved, because privacy intrusions are occurring in the hope of demonstrating their value after the event.[5]

Another fundamental problem with computer matching is that it breaches the privacy principles held in law throughout the world. One of the most important of these principles demands that information supplied for one purpose should not be used for another purpose unless the individual concerned has given consent. An indication of how fundamentally ineffective the law can be on this issue is the sad reality that the law provides exemptions if the scheme in question can turn a dollar for the government. In this case, computer matching would be clearly exempted from many of the conditions of the *Commonwealth Privacy Act*.

One of the most dangerous long-term outcomes of a data-matching program is that it tends to encourage governments to create a universal population numbering system. Since the greatest practical problem for computer matching is the various ways people identify themselves, such a numbering scheme would be most attractive. It would save the trouble and expense of maintaining many numbering systems.

Even in the absence of a single national number, the data-matching programs, if fully linked, can create the effect of a single number. Data matching can contain processes to merge various numbering systems, applying criteria for determining whether a number from one sector adequately matches a number from another. There is, in effect, a "working number" or "working identity" applied or created by the data-matching system.

The second key area of concern relates to the accuracy of the information being matched. The key assumption underlying any data-matching program is that information from each of the sources is parallel and compatible. Such is never the case. Even apparently identical items of information or categories often have different meanings in different systems. Such terms as "de facto", "marriage", "child", "dependent", "spouse", "income", "living costs", "permanent" and "temporary" can be and are used in different ways by different departments, and people often quite legitimately use them differently according to a changed circumstance. A person's information may also quite legitimately vary between departments because of the date the information was originally provided. Data matching may not take these discrepancies into account when determining if a person's file is a "hit". The decisions are made on a clinical basis, with the computer-matching staff being unaware of the broader context of each case.

Once a person has been "flagged" (marked for scrutiny) by the system, it is invariably the case that the onus of proof of innocence is on the person rather than the government. Once an investigation proceeds, information that may be wrong or out of date is then liable to be communicated to people with no direct involvement in the case, resulting in possible harm or embarrassment to the file subject.

The Department of Social Security gave evidence to the Inquiry into Fraud on the Commonwealth that in one data-matching exercise, action was taken against only 61 of 2334 people under investigation for fraud. Presumably, the other 2273 people were investigated without just cause.

In October 1990 the New South Wales Council of Civil Liberties gave evidence to a Senate Committee[6] that false accusation was occurring because of computer matching. One man received a letter from the Australian Tax Office advising that his entire refund had been withheld by the department because of outstanding child-support liabilities. The crime had been detected by the computer-matching process. The only problem was that this victim had never had any children.

The Child Support scheme matching process is a small-time operation compared to the major matching programs operated by the DSS and the Tax Office. In one program alone, where 9,000,000 DSS records were computer matched against 1,000,000 Department of Employment, Education and Training (DEET) records, 65,000 individuals were identified for further investigation.[7] The department has not released details of the number of people, if any, that have been prosecuted.

One of the most alarming aspects of widespread data matching is that it gives the technical ability to develop a comprehensive profile of each member of the population. The mere fact that at the push of a button a detailed profile is possible should set alarm bells ringing in the ears of a population tuned to the dangers of an ID card.

A United Nations study entitled *Human Rights and Scientific and Technological Development* warns:

> ... the increased expansion of computerisation of personal data may result in a "dossier society" which would have "dehumanising" effects on the individual. The relative inflexibility of computer based record keeping resulting from the computers having been designed to use certain preconceived categories, coupled with the constraints that some computerised systems put on the freedom of persons concerned to provide explanatory details in responding to questions, have been considered as contributing to the dehumanising effect of computerisation.[8]

The Australian Government has placed a great deal of emphasis on the absence of a central database in the computer matching program. In response to this claim Roger Clarke, Associate Professor in the Department of Commerce at the Australian National University, studied the draft specifications in the Federal LEAN tender documents for the supply of computer equipment, and concluded:

> Any claims that the scheme involves no central register are dispelled by the Draft Specification's references to data maintenance and updating of the matched record in "the large file," (6.3.4.1), the loading of changed records (7.9.1), large volume historical data (8.2), future requirements for transaction processing (8.3), and "the National Database" (8.5). It is intended that data be not merely received and matched, and then discarded; the data is also to be stored and updated. There will therefore be an ongoing "master-file", maintained by a single agency in one location, which is what is meant by the term "central register".[9]

In the same paper Clarke goes on to assess the likely magnitude of the computer-matching proposals:

A *total of* **10 million separate individuals** *would appear to be the subject of records held by the system (6.3.4.1), although the same paragraph mentions another master-file of 7 million records ... Current holdings of historical data are stated to be over 60 gigabytes (8.2) — which would be 300 million records if they averaged 200 bytes; and this is presumably before large-scale accumulation of data from multiple sources is commenced.*

The above tender for the matching scheme also indicated that the proposal would ultimately "accommodate an environment of double, then treble the initial size over one to two years". Not only does it appear from the tender documents and from expert analysis that the government has provided a misleading assessment of the data-matching plans, but the government's assurances seem to miss the point intentionally. The essential issue is that data matching creates the effect of a single computer even if no single master computer exists.

To understand this fundamental point, you only have to think of a computer as a mass of separate parts, each of which can communicate in a set way with the other parts. A large computer, in fact, is many smaller computers all communicating in harmony. Data matching is an extension of this process. The matching process allows one computer to talk easily with others, thus creating one giant computer.

This, perhaps more than any single point, is the one that should be foremost in the minds of our more aware and sensitive politicians. Data matching is not just a more efficient way for computers to speak; **it is the systematic development of a vast, multi-faceted database that reaches into every aspect of our lives**. It is not good enough for a government to artfully engineer semantics and to use moral blackmail to achieve compliance. A government should think beyond the gains of the moment to consider what sort of society it is helping to create. Privacy advocates have always been deeply concerned that to link computers will create a set of community and political norms which are inimical to a free society.

This dataveillance is likely to produce a chilling effect on the population. This chill comes about when people feel they are under constant surveillance. It is, in many ways, similar to the "environment of deterrence" philosophy favoured by many police forces. Once this emotion has set in, it is difficult to reverse. This same impact was predicted for the Australia Card. Data matching will produce a similar effect, but its impact will take some years to manifest.

The government argues that the dangers of this data-matching epidemic are counterbalanced by big monetary returns. However, the promises of a financial bonanza have not always materialised. Extensions to the Tax File Number scheme were to have collected over a billion dollars a year, but in May 1992 the government revised this estimate since they had suffered a shortfall of a massive 750 million dollars, undermining the credibility of the TFN scheme.[10] As well, data-matching schemes that were to reap $340 million in 1991-92, brought the government only $35 million.[11]

The expected cost benefit of these systems should be a key factor in the debate about whether the computer-matching schemes are in the public interest. If a scheme produces a billion dollars, then the public is likely to view it as valuable. Privacy concerns might be readily traded off for a return of that magnitude. A return of twenty million dollars, however, might be seen as insufficient to outweigh the dangers.

Sadly, almost no figures are available relating to computer matching. The Australian Tax Office "conservatively" estimated the return from LEAN at twenty million dollars per year.[12] The Privacy Commissioners' 1992 report on data matching gives no figures, and leaves to the individual departments the decision about whether financial aspects of the system should be made public.

RAISING OBJECTIONS TO COMPUTER MATCHING

In mid-1991, members of the Australian Privacy Foundation wrote to the Privacy Commissioner, complaining that the LEAN proposal was a major threat to the privacy of Australians, and that it breached the Privacy Act.[13] The commissioner wrote back saying that there were real questions about whether he had power to take any action. Fourteen months later, at the time of writing, action has yet to be taken on the Privacy Foundation's complaint, despite its request for an urgent resolution of the matter. With the sole exception of a short letter advising that the commissioner would "investigate" the matter, the foundation has received no correspondence with regard to its complaint.

In its submission to the 1992 House of Representatives Inquiry into Fraud on the Commonwealth, the foundation stated that it was "deeply dissatisfied" by this situation. The foundation went on to say, "This question should have been resolved at least a year ago, and yet it is still the subject of dispute behind closed doors. We have made a legitimate complaint under s.36 (1) of the Privacy Act. The commissioner has, in our view, failed to act with either the speed or the tenacity required by the urgency of the situation." And continued, "We are dismayed by what appears to be the paralysis of the commissioner on this matter. It is regrettable that the commissioner is unable to resolve a pivotal complaint on a matter as crucial as the LEAN system."

The Privacy Commissioner has said little about the LEAN proposal, and far from distancing himself from the scheme has appointed a member of his staff to act on his behalf as an observer on the steering committee of the project. His involvement in the project has been used by the Attorney-General's Department as an implied endorsement of the scheme, "The Department has consulted the Privacy Commissioner on the project and invited him to participate in the formulation of the necessary operational safeguards."[14]

The Privacy Foundation has received dozens of written requests for it to represent the concerns of people in New South Wales, but can do nothing directly. Advice from the Privacy Commissioner's office is that complaints cannot be dealt with until the system has commenced.

In its submission to the fraud inquiry, the foundation said, "The Commonwealth has also behaved in a reprehensible manner. The LEAN system has been constructed outside of the authority of law, and entirely in secret. No public consultation has taken place, and a gag appears to have been placed on public comment by departments."

THE GLOBAL CONTEXT

Within the next ten years, all the world's major computers will be able to communicate with each other. A telecommunications computer in Ohio will be able to talk with a bank computer in Brussels; Russian defence computers will be replaced (using Western dollars) with conventional systems that are designed to link with computers in Europe and America.

The taxation systems of all developed countries will use compatible hardware and software, as will the computers of all communications and immigration agencies. Police agencies world-wide are already making their choices of systems on the basis of their ability to communicate easily with police computers of other national and international law enforcement organisations.

A trend is emerging internationally for nations to reach agreement on the transfer and exchange of information stored on these systems. It may be only a matter of time before the computer-matching epidemic touches every facet of human activity in every part of the globe.

COMPUTER-MATCHING PROGRAMS IN AUSTRALIA

By October 1990, there were 31 active and proposed major data-matching programs involving Commonwealth Government departments These are, in summary:

Name of program	Agencies involved
Apprenticeship allowance checks	DEET and DIR
AUSTUDY and enrolments	DEET and educational institutions
AUSTUDY, DSS pensions and benefits	DEET and DSS
Benefits checks	DSS and insurance company payments
Benefits checks	DSS employment declarations and ATO
Benefits entitlement	DSS and HIC
Benefits entitlement	DSS, land titles offices and local government
Benefits entitlement	DSS and state corrective services departments
Benefits identification	DSS and AEO
Benefits identification	DSS and overseas welfare authorities

Name of program	Agencies involved
Benefits identification	DSS and state Registrar-General offices and HIC
Child-support checks	DSS and Child Support Agency
Criminal investigation	DSS, AEO, state Registrar-General's offices and HIC
DEET/employment income match	DEET and DEET-subsidised employers
DSS accelerated claims	DSS intra-agency
Income-matching system	ATO, employers and investment bodies
Insurance claim checks	DSS and Australia Post
Insurance claim checks	DSS and Comcare
Insurance claim checks	DSS and insurance company records
Insurance claim checks	DSS and Telecom
Overseas student matches	DEET and DILGEA
Overseas students/student assistance	DEET and DILGEA
Pensioner match	DSS and DVA
Pensions/income match	ATO, DVA and DSS
Prescribed payments/ unemployment	DSS and ATO
Sales tax returns	ATO and ACS
Social security and payroll	DSS and Department of Finance
Social service benefits/ departures	DSS and DILGEA
Student assistance/income match	ATO and DEET
Student assistance/pensions	DEET and DSS
Veterans' pensions/ superannuation	DVA and superannuation funds

Source: Privacy Commissioner's Draft Data Matching Guidelines, 1990.

PRIVACY INTERNATIONAL
RESOLUTION 1.2 —
CONCERNING THE ESTABLISHMENT BY THE
AUSTRALIAN GOVERNMENT OF A MAJOR
INVESTIGATIVE DATABASE

RECOGNIZING THAT THE AUSTRALIAN GOVERNMENT is now considering the development of a comprehensive database containing personal information;

FURTHER recognizing that the Government of Australia is a signatory to the OECD convention on data protection, and has established a commitment to protecting the right to privacy:

THE PARTICIPANTS OF THIS MEETING OF PRIVACY INTERNATIONAL express concern about the Australian Government's proposed Law Enforcement Access Network, especially with regard to:

1. The lack of any prior consultative process
2. The breadth of usage intended
3. The contention that no privacy issues are involved in respect of publicly available information, and
4. The exclusion of database containing personal information from perview of the Privacy Commissioner

PRIVACY INTERNATIONAL respectfully calls on the Australian Government:

1. To withdraw the proposal
2. To instruct the agency involved to prepare and publish a privacy impact statement, and
3. To instigate public hearings

NOTES

1. Roger Clarke, "Computer Matching", unpublished paper, 31 March 1991.
2. L. B. Weiss "Government steps up use of computer matching to find fraud in programs", Weekly Report *Congressional Quarterly*, 26 February, 1983. Office of Technology Assessment "Federal Government Information technology. Electronic record systems and individual privacy" OTA-Cit 296, US Government Printing Office, Washington DC, June 1986.

3. Evidence and submission of Australian Privacy Foundation to the House of Representatives Standing Committee on Banking, Finance and Public Administration Fraud Sub-committee, *Hansard*, 17 July 1992.

4. *Ibid.*

5. House of Representatives Standing Committee on Banking, Finance and Public Administration Fraud Sub-Committee, Submission of the Privacy Commissioner, *Hansard*, 28 May 1992, pp. 3, 6.

6. Standing Committee on Legal and Constitutional Affairs (Senate), *Hansard*, 19 October 1990.

7. Privacy Commission, *1991 Annual Report*, p. 46.

8. Cited in Roger Clarke, *Computer Matching*, draft analysis paper (unpublished) Australian National University, Canberra, 31 March 1991.

9. The numbers in these quotes relate to sections of the tender documents.

10. *Sydney Morning Herald*, 19 May 1992.

11. *Australian Financial Review*, 29 August 1992.

12. House of Representatives Standing Committee on Banking, Finance and Public Administration Fraud Sub-Committee, *Hansard*, 17 July 1992.

13. 8 June 1991.

14. House of Representatives Standing Committee on Banking, Finance and Public Administration Fraud Sub-Committee, Submission of the Attorney-General's Department, *Hansard*, 28 May 1992, p. 28.

CHAPTER SIX

THE HOUSE
OF CARDS

"Like the innocent small town invaded in a monster movie, all those people work and play, unaware of how fragile and vulnerable their community is. It could be destroyed outright by a virus, or worse, it could consume itself with mutual suspicion, tangle itself up in locks, security checkpoints and surveillance, wither away by becoming so inaccessible and bureaucratic that no-one would want it anymore."

Clifford Stoll, *The Cuckoo's Egg.*[1]

The date is a Tuesday sometime in the very near future, and in the Dutch city of Utrecht, a respectable-looking young man walks into the computer laboratory of a research institute affiliated with his university. Using a fellow student's pass code to operate the system, he accesses the huge Datanet 1 public computer network. On the pretext of sending a series of chemical formulae to another computer lab in Amsterdam, he loads into his terminal a disk on which he has placed a computer virus.

Viruses are custom-made computer programs (programs are sets of instructions that operate computers) designed to disrupt or even destroy a computer system. Such programs are not uncommon, but this one is special. Known as a "stealth worm", this virus boasts artificial intelligence and has a structure similar to DNA. It is possibly the most dangerous computer virus ever devised.

This intense man watches as two years of programming effort come to life in the terminal, and travel out over the public network, bringing hundreds of computers throughout the Netherlands to a sudden crash.

The worm is transmitted from the Rotterdam computer installation to other international transmission and exchange centres, and it rapidly infects other major public data networks. Via the X25 and X75 gateways, where computer transmission signals are processed, the stealth worm spreads rapidly through the Tymmet, Telenet, Infonet and Compuserve networks. As the business day begins in the eastern United States, the worm reaches the teleport serving New York City, and within 15 minutes causes a crash of the Clearinghouse for Interbank Payments Systems (CHIPS), the Federal Reserve Network, the New York Stock Exchange and American Stock Exchange automatic trading systems, and New York's automatic teller machine (ATM) network. Rapidly, the national payments system is brought to a standstill, and the US macro-economy is dealt a severe blow. The worm spreads so rapidly that within another 20 minutes every automatic teller machine, bank computer and stock exchange system throughout the USA is halted. The Canadian stock-trading system is also infected, and the Canadian economy is then similarly paralysed.

Meanwhile, in Europe, the worm penetrates the key regional networks in Brussels, and creates a major crisis. Every computer system in Belgium is infected with the worm. One small security flaw allows the worm to penetrate the huge Society for Worldwide Interbank Financial Telecommunications (SWIFT) mainframe. The worm quickly spreads to infect every banking computer in the world. The economies of every nation are paralysed. From Brussels and Datanet 1, the worm invades the European Community's network, and spreads itself, paralysing every networked computer in Europe. The worm accesses the West German and Austrian Data-P network and halts the processing of oil prices in Vienna. The oil market collapses. Gold-pricing in Johannesburg is also paralysed. The world's monetary infrastructure collapses. By the start of the Japanese business day, all financial transactions have had to be suspended, a state of affairs that is replicated throughout Asia and the Far East.

Some interconnections of networks permit the worm to access sensitive government computer networks around the world. Within hours, the command, control, intelligence and communications capabilities of the world's major powers are severely diminished. Economies start to collapse. There is talk of war.

Less than 16 hours have passed since the worm was introduced into a Dutch terminal. None of the standard defences has stood a chance of working against the worm. No one part of the financial system dares disconnect from the networks, because to do so would cause massive damage to the industry causing the currency or stock index to plunge. And there would never be any hope of voluntarily shutting down the entire international finance system to stop the spread of the worm. Ultimately, the virus infects most of the world's networked computers, with little hope of the virus ever being exorcised.

THE PROBLEMS OF A WORLD-WIDE COMPUTER NETWORK

The above scenario, originally suggested by US security expert Wayne Madsen,[2] may sound like fantasy, but most computer-security professionals agree that in principle such a crisis is possible. All that would be required is the right program.

The right program will depend on the existence of three factors: knowledge of the security procedures in the world's major computer networks; money and resources to develop and unleash the right stealth worm; and the malicious motivation to disrupt the world's computer systems.

The motivation already exists. Countless terrorist organisations, anarchist groups, revolutionaries, hackers and crackers all have reasons to inflict damage.

There is a view — and it is one that is gaining widespread acceptance — that computers and computer terrorism will replace conventional terrorism, just as the predictions of a few years ago that computer-based fraud would eclipse standard crimes such as bank robbery have already become reality. The difference between mere computer fraud and network-virus terrorism, however, is that the latter threatens the stability of entire nations, and ultimately the relationship between nations. Indeed, as the stealth worm scenario demonstrates, on a financial and political level, virus terrorism is no less a threat than the spectre of nuclear warfare.

The world's financial system now depends on the intricate interlinking of trillions of microchips. Transactions are calculated to hundredths of a second, and fortunes can be lost in less than the time it takes to push a button. Major multi-national corporations depend as much as the corner small business on the proper functioning of information technology. The lives and fortunes of hundreds of millions of people are tied inexorably to their computer terminals.

HOW DOES THE WORM FUNCTION?

The emerging threat to the world's computers comes in many forms — trapdoors, logic bombs, worms, viruses and Trojan horses. All variations are malicious computer programs, deliberately designed to infect and sometimes completely destroy computer systems.

The programmer who creates the worm constructs a complex series of instructions similar in some ways to the instructions encoded in DNA or a biological virus. Most worms start by hiding in a computer's existing software, waiting for a particular date or an event, before coming to life, corrupting the hard disk of the machines, or instructing the host computer to do the same. More than a thousand key viruses have so far been detected, and more than fifty new strains are being found each month throughout the world.

Many of the people behind these viruses are new frontier criminals; usually male, between the ages of 16 and 25, and right on the cutting edge of computer software development. Some produce the viruses as no more than an intellectual challenge; others do so because of a particular motivation or goal. An "AIDS" virus uncovered in 1989 was designed to blackmail the recipients of complimentary computer programs to pay money to a Panama postal address. The complimentary programs had been sent on disk to 20,000 computer operators, but much to the horror of the recipients, the "AIDS" program, rather than being an educational program as they had thought, was a lethal Trojan horse virus, a time bomb that would ultimately destroy all data on the computer system.[3] The architect of the virus was eventually tracked down and jailed, but not before a great deal of damage was inflicted and a large amount of money was expended.

The new hackers and crackers have developed an extraordinary intelligence network. They use nation-wide and trans-national electronic bulletin boards to swap information on security systems, and ways to break them. Networks, or electronic communities, of virus writers are forming around the world. Vital and often confidential program information is posted and distributed through these networks.

Hackers in the United States even have a glossy magazine called *2600 — the Hacker Quarterly*, containing articles with such titles as "Secret Frequencies", "Hacker News", "Build a tone tracer" and "Magnetic stripes (how to copy them)". Considerable amounts of sensitive information about computer security systems are freely circulated around the hacker community, many of whom believe that corporations and governments are the real criminals who deserve to be brought to justice. Information networks are commonly interpreted as either the new heart of international socialism, or the engine room of capitalism. A great many viruses are unleashed onto systems because of the program writer's hatred of what the network stands for.

In 1991 Richard Hollinger, of the Department of Sociology of the University of Florida, told the Computers, Freedom and Privacy Conference in San Francisco: "To them [the young computer hackers] pirating software, sharing passwords, illegally accessing remote computers, browsing through electronic files, is not deviate behaviour. Instead, the real 'criminals' in the world of computers are the private corporations, institutions and government agencies who wish to deny them access to this wealth of information."

It is difficult for many members of the older generations to comprehend what has been spawned by the computer revolution of the past decade. We often admire how much faster, or bigger, or smarter information technology has become. But more significant in privacy issues and harder to grasp is the quantum shift in human attitudes and values that this technology engenders. Millions of youngsters around the world nowadays live in a different life matrix, a sort of computer network reality, a virtual reality where tangibility is confirmed through prompts, flags, and program instructions. An entire generation of young people sees reality and change in terms of networks and network communications. Older people might complain that video is keeping their kids indoors. Well, computer networks are achieving the effect of confining young people to a terminal, but they also liberate their movements in time and space. These youngsters have inherited a new dimension known as "cyberspace". In the US they call it "living on the net". This new lifestyle pushes forward an electronic frontier no less impressive than the old pioneer frontiers of the eighteenth century.

Many hackers believe that the technology of the present and future will not bring a new and glorious prosperity for everyone. One of Australia's leading computer experts, Roger Clarke of the Australian National University, believes that the end result of rampant technology will be anarchy. He says this will happen because the new richness and availability of information will prompt attacks upon social institutions. As the institutions respond with ever more repressive measures to defend themselves, the community might then take possibly violent action to remove them.[4]

Little wonder, with such knowledge and passion behind them, that the new generation of viruses and worms are so effecive.

The stealth worm is the most dangerous virus yet devised. Once introduced into a computer system or network, the stealth worm issues instructions to the computer to hide its presence. This means that even though a computer operator constantly scans the computer to see whether there is any program space unacounted for (which may indicate a hidden virus), the stealth worm will instruct the computer to lie. The virus then reproduces itself, travelling through and between networks, leaving a ghost of itself at each new point. At the appropriate moment, the worm will destroy the system it has infected.

HOW IS THE WORM USED?

There are numerous examples of malicious worm and virus attacks on computer networks. In November 1988, a Cornell University student devised and released a particularly vicious and fast worm which succeeded in shutting down, or "crashing", thousands of computer systems throughout the United States. Defence networks, as well as the National Science Foundation's vast and influential resource and information network, were also infected.[5] Another virus introduced via electronic mail in 1987 gridlocked and infected hundreds of IBM mainframe computers around the world.[6] On a smaller scale, an American financial company suffered an infection in July 1991, shutting down 2200 computers for a week. In Sydney, a major bank recently shut down its entire dealing network on the mere suspicion that a virus had entered its system.[7]

In Australia, the threat of the Michelangelo virus caused widespread concern amongst corporations, and persuaded some companies to either doctor their programs or paralysed completely on the great artist's birthday.

Telecommunications systems are particularly vulnerable to virus attack. On 15 January 1990, American Telephone and Telegraph (AT&T), one of America's major telephone companies, suffered a major virus attack that virtually shut down its national network.

The crisis first became apparent in AT&T's long-distance control room 80 kilometres west of New York City. Here huge video maps of the United States cover an entire wall, and are illuminated by countless green lights, indicating that the network is functioning satisfactorily. At 2.30 p.m., the lights started changing to red, indicating that the network was breaking down. Tens of thousands of customers were failing to get their calls through.

The crisis had begun when Switching Computer number 50 in New York found a small but unidentified error in its software, and automatically took itself off the network to reboot (switch on again). The computer first notified the other switching facilities that it intended to go off-line, and its calls were thus diverted elsewhere in the network. Once the New York computer had re-established itself (a process that took less than two seconds) it sent out an "OK" message to other facilities, which then reset their routing tables accordingly. So far so good.

However, a domino effect was then sparked when the virus in the New York computer caused the OK message to be re-sent. This threw all other computers in the network into a spin, triggering their shut-down. As they came back on-line, the same bug caused them to issue multiple OK messages, compounding the network's collapse.

Within 10 minutes, all 114 switching stations were affected, and 50 per cent of calls on the world's largest and most sophisticated communications system were unable to connect.

Although the technical problems were largely resolved by the following night, the damage to AT&T was incalculable. The tangible loss for the day was US$75 million, but the overall effect on the company's business was far greater, as rival companies quickly exploited the damage that the failure caused to AT&T's reputation.[8]

The chance of such a major catastrophe occurring on an international basis in the key computer systems is still considered remote, but Jim Bates, a leading British computer-virus expert recently warned "My experience is that speculation from 12 months ago is beginning to become reality".[9]

One very clear example of vulnerability can be seen in the world's satellite control systems. Although the main satellite control systems are invariably mainframe computers, and thus less likely than personal computers (PCs) to be infiltrated by viruses, the satellite tracking stations are not: they are connected to PCs. A worm or other virus can infiltrate these tracking systems and, just by slowing the mechanism minutely can change the path of a satellite. As the world's telecommunications organisations move to universal personal numbering systems, in which people can be tracked anywhere in the world, satellite integrity will become even more vital.[10]

WHY THE GLOBAL CRISIS WILL AFFECT PRIVACY

This gloomy sequence of events has important ramifications for privacy. There can be little doubt that the computer virus will soon be regarded as the single greatest threat to the stability of the international economy. As the world moves toward one compatible, integrated computer canopy, the vulnerability of the system will increase.[11] As the vulnerability increases, opportunities for terrorism will also become more apparent.

As the world and everyone in it becomes more dependent on sensitive and vulnerable computer systems, the need to protect them may well override the rights of users and, eventually, the rights of everyone. The United States Government is attempting to pass legislation to allow routine and mass surveillance of all computer communication, partly in an attempt to monitor information that may threaten computer networks.[12]

To minimise the possibility of terrorist attacks or sabotage, governments may well demand more and more access to our personal computers and our communications. It is not unfeasible, as has been suggested in the United States, that a government-issued identity card containing an individual's biological details would be needed in order to enter computer systems. In this scenario, everyone who wanted to access any computer network would have to use a card which verified (through fingerprints or eye scans) that they were who they said they were. This would make it easier for the police to track down any malicious action. As more and more people need to access these networks either because of their work or their day-to-day business, a compulsory national or international biometric smart card is quite feasible.

In the United States, privacy advocates are concerned that law-enforcement agencies will impose invasive initiatives to track down virus writers and control the flow of information within computer systems and networks. There is a widespread fear that if the stakes are high enough, governments will invoke anti-terrorism powers that will override civil rights.[13] The government has already sought through Congress to require that communication service providers make available the "plain text" version of encrypted (coded) computer communications. This effort was successfully opposed by privacy advocates, and computer and communications companies, but the FBI and other agencies continue to work to those ends.[14] If we are not allowed to even communicate privately, and to speak in a way that protects our privacy, one important plank of individual rights is destroyed. Cryptography will remain one of the battlegrounds for communications privacy for the foreseeable future.[15]

Law enforcement has always been one of the greatest threats to privacy and rights. The efforts to maintain national security in its battle with terrorism give law enforcement extraordinary scope for intrusion. Computer terrorism is likely to provide this opportunity. Political groups which have traditionally depended on brutality to exercise their intentions, may take the option of going down the technological road. If, for example, some practical aspects of regional collaboration are made possible through computer linkage, it's only natural that enemies of collaboration will direct their energies to destroying the computer facilities. And since the facilities are frequently well protected, the damage must be achieved through the system itself.

In the eyes of law-enforcement agencies, every computer user is a potential hacker, and therefore a potential threat. The executive editor of the American-based *PC Magazine*, Gus Venditto, believes that no special genius is required to develop and launch a computer virus: "Any programmer could make a virus. There are maybe 300,000 programmers in the world who could do it if they wanted to do it, pretty simply."

The development of the global computer canopy has the potential to make aspects of our lifestyle more fruitful and productive. It clearly also has the potential to create an international police state in which access to the network is essential for survival, but dependent on the surrender of privacy and rights.

NOTES

1. Clifford Stoll, *The Cuckoo's Egg*, Bodley Head, London, 1989, p. 323.
2. This scenario was originally published in *Information Age*, vol. 11, no. 3, 3 July 1989, pp. 131–137.
3. *Sydney Morning Herald*, 26 October 1991, p. 42.
4. Closing session of the Shaping Organisations, Shaping Technology (SOST) Conference, Adelaide, 1991.
5. *Information Age*, ibid.
6. *Ibid.*
7. Peter Huck, "Tracking down the computer terrorists", *Sydney Morning Herald*, 26 October 1991, p. 42.
8. David Davies, "Anatomy of a disaster", *Computer Law and Security Report*, Jul–Aug 1991.
9. *Sydney Morning Herald*, 26 October 1991, p. 42.
10. Motorola's Iridium project will place 77 satellites in orbit for this purpose.
11. The development of Open Systems planning means that computers in many different environments will have the capacity to communicate fully with each other.
12. Bill s.266 of 1991 specified that people encrypting (encoding) their communications through the computer networks had to tell the government how to unscramble the code.
13. See the proceedings of the first Computers, Freedom and Privacy Conference, San Francisco, 1991. IEEE Computer Society Press, Los Alamitos, California, 1991.
14. The FBI has already placed another bill before the Senate which would require telecommunications companies to ensure that all technology can be intercepted by law-enforcement agencies. This is currently being opposed by the civil liberties lobby.
15. See *Proceedings of 1991 Cryptography and Privacy Conference, Washington DC, June 1991*. National Academy Press, 1991.

CHAPTER SEVEN

CREDIT FILES

"A pig bought on credit is forever grunting"

Spanish Proverb

Every time you apply for credit, whether from a credit union, a building society or a retail store, your personal details are checked against a massive computer database controlled by the finance industry. Ten million Australians, and the entire finance sector, rely on this computer to provide details of credit worthiness. This massive bank of information is in the hands of a private organisation called the Credit Reference Association of Australia (CRAA).

When the CRAA began its operations in 1968, it was little more than a humble effort at stitching together a credible database of credit histories for the New South Wales finance industry. By the late 1980s, the organisation had grown into a massive national operation which had collected files on 10 million Australians and more than a million businesses. Over time, membership of the CRAA — whether intentionally or not — was opened up to virtually anyone in the commercial sector — insurers, real estate companies, hire companies, private investigators and mercantile agents.

Originally established for the use of the finance industry, this giant information sieve provided services to just about anyone who claimed an interest in seeing personal credit histories. By 1989 the CRAA had 5000 members accessing the CRAA database from an estimated 13,000 locations at the rate of 25,000 file accesses per day.[1]

Until the late 1980s, the CRAA based its files on "negative reporting", that is, a credit file whose main feature was the notification of a bad debt or bankruptcy. Then, the association decided that it would massively expand its file base by incorporating not just a person's bad payments, but all payments. Thus a credit file would become a payment and credit profile, showing the precise payment performance of a debtor.

This scheme, known as positive reporting, caused a storm of protest amongst privacy and consumer advocates. Senator Nick Bolkus, federal Minister for Consumer Affairs at the time, told the Senate that the scheme involved collecting so much information that it could create a detailed personal profile on Australians, regardless of whether or not they had defaulted on a debt.[2]

In April 1989 the Australian Privacy Foundation convened a summit meeting to discuss the proposals. Members of Parliament from all parties attended, as did representatives of the finance industry, the CRAA, and consumer groups. Some sectors of the finance industry made a last-minute attempt to boycott the meeting, but this failed to have a serious effect on events. The finance industry put its case to the meeting, but failed to convince many of the politicians and community groups that the scheme was in the public interest. Indeed, as more information was revealed about the history of the CRAAs expansion, and the proposed positive reporting scheme, the concern expressed by consumer and privacy groups increased. Senator Bolkus left the meeting and told waiting media that the government would pass legislation to control the activities of credit-reporting agencies.

Few people would deny the need for a credit-reporting industry. Every day around 50,000 people in Australia apply for credit in one form or another,[3] and outstanding consumer debt now stands at around 40 billion dollars.

Privacy and consumer organisations were by no means in agreement over the issue. Financial counsellors were nervous about moves to restrict the use of credit files. Their argument was that the credit-reference system performed the valid function of limiting the amount of financial over-commitment in the community. While the privacy lobby agreed that this might be so, its response was that the bad outweighed the good. The abuses of the credit-reporting system, coupled with the general community-wide surveillance caused by positive reporting, could not be justified through the occasional reduction of indebtedness.

Over the following eighteen months, the finance industry waged an extensive campaign to convince the Parliament and the public that legislation would be counter-productive and costly. Some of the campaigning was conducted from the Canberra parliamentary offices of front bench Liberal members. The industry claimed that the new laws would cost consumers two billion dollars a year,[4] though the mathematics behind this figure remain to this day a mystery even to the most gifted of economists. Representatives of the finance industry, under the newly acquired umbrella of the Credit Reporting Forum met with the then Prime Minister, Bob Hawke, to appeal against the legislation, but he rejected their arguments. The industry managed to have the issue raised a second time in Cabinet, which also rejected the appeal. Politicians in Canberra had sensed that the public were in favour of laws to control credit reporting, even if it meant the move might result in a financial cost to the consumer.

Responding to the finance industry's protests about the costs of the proposal, the Australian Privacy Foundation observed, "If the finance industry wishes to curb civil rights on the basis of cost, it may well propose that we should send kids back down the mines".[5]

It was not simply the spectre of positive reporting, however, that drove the government into action. The membership of the Credit Reference Association was far too broad. Members in 1989 included television hire companies, employment agencies, private investigators, mercantile agents, utilities (gas and electric companies), builders, insurance companies, real estate agencies, couriers, legal firms, credit card companies, retailers, finance companies, arilines, hotels, stock exchanges, government departments, laboratories and car hire companies. (A great many of these kinds of business still retain membership of the Credit Reference Association.)

The problem was that if you were wrongly accused by just one of these organisations, or were in dispute over a debt, your credit standing with all other organisations would have been adversely affected. A problem with a television hire company might have made it impossible to rent a house. Such a situation was deplored by privacy advocates, who lobbied for a law to restrict such a wide access to credit files.

However, the *Privacy (Credit Reporting) Amendment Act 1990* gave Australians, for the first time, national and legally enforceable privacy rights concerning credit information, which are detailed below. The Act came into force on 24 September 1991.

The credit industry claimed that the legislation was the most restrictive in the Western world, and, certainly that it rolled back the clock on some of the most objectionable aspects of the use of credit bureaus, particularly by prohibiting their use by the insurance industry, real estate agents, mercantile agents, government licensing bodies, Telecom and others who were not providing credit. Despite these advances, the legislation leaves most normal aspects of credit reporting unaffected, and contains a number of undesirable loopholes which could allow improper practices to continue.

It must be said, however, that the CRAA is a predominantly ethical organisation that appears to play a fairly straight bat. Whether or not loopholes exist in the new law, it is unlikely that the association will intentionally exploit them to the maximum extent.

Much of the detailed control of credit reporting was left by Parliament to the Privacy Commissioner, who was to draw up a legally enforceable code of conduct, to come into effect at the same time as the Act.

The credit industry succeeded in having Federal Parliament enact last-minute changes to the new credit-reporting law.[6] The changes meant that most of the Act, including the code of conduct, did not come into force on the scheduled starting date of 24 September 1991, but was delayed until 25 February 1992. The amended law was not as strict as the old Bill and allowed some industries (for example, trade insurers) to use credit reports.

WHAT INFORMATION CAN BE PUT ONTO YOUR CREDIT FILE?

The information contained in your file is now strictly governed by law. The following items can be included.

1. Information that is reasonably necessary to identify you (full name, known aliases, sex, date of birth, two immediately previous addresses, current or last-known employer and driver's licence number);
2. a record of an inquiry to the credit bureau made by a credit provider (bank or finance company, et cetera) in connection with your application for credit, together with the amount of credit sought;
3. a record of an inquiry about you made by a mortgage insurer in connection with mortgage insurance;
4. a record of an inquiry made about you by a trade insurer in connection with trade insurance in respect of your application for commercial credit;

5. a record of an inquiry made by a credit provider about a guarantor for a loan;
6. the name of a credit provider with whom you have a current account;
7. a record of credit in respect of which you are overdue by more than 60 days and for which steps have been taken by the credit provider to recover all or part of the amount outstanding;
8. a record of a cheque for at least $100 which you have drawn and which has been presented and dishonoured twice;
9. court judgements and bankruptcy orders made against you;
10. a credit provider's opinion that you have committed, in the circumstances specified, a serious credit infringement (a serious credit infringement occurs when a person has fraudulently obtained credit or has fraudulently evaded obligations to repay the debt. Overdue payments do not constitute a serious infringement.);
11. a statement provided by you describing a correction, deletion or addition which you have sought to make to the information on your file;
12. a record of any disclosures of your file made by the credit-reporting agency; or
13. a note to the effect that you are no longer overdue in your payments, or that you contend that you are not overdue.

It has also been agreed in the Privacy Commissioner's consultations with the credit industry that some sort of notation for the account type should be included in the credit file.

WHAT INFORMATION IS PROHIBITED?

- Race, ethnic or national origin
- Criminal or police record information
- Political, social or religious beliefs, membership or affiliations
- Medical history, physical or mental conditions or handicaps
- Sexual practices or preferences
- Lifestyle, character or reputation

In accordance with the principles of the Privacy Act, the Credit Reference Association can keep only information that is relevant to credit provision.

HOW LONG CAN CREDIT AGENCIES KEEP PERSONAL INFORMATION?

From September 1992, credit bureaus are permitted to keep personal information on file for a specified period only, after which the information must be deleted. The maximum periods are:

1. enquiries by credit providers, mortgage insurers and trade insurers — five years from the date of the inquiry;
2. a record that a credit provider is no longer a current credit provider — fourteen days after the credit agency is notified of the change of status;
3. information about overdue payments — five years;
4. information about dishonoured cheques — five years;
5. information about court judgements — five years after the date of judgement;
6. information about bankruptcy orders — seven years after the date of the order; and
7. serious credit infringement believed to have been committed by you — seven years from notification.

As a rule, files which have been inactive for five years are deleted.

HOW TO GET ACCESS TO YOUR CREDIT FILE

You have the right to receive a copy of your credit file. To do this you will need to write to the CRAA and provide details that will be sufficient to establish your identity. As there are many millions of files, it is likely there will be several people with your exact name and, possibly, even your date of birth. Current and previous addresses will be essential, but it is important to remember that information supplied in this form may be included in your file.

The credit agency is no longer allowed to charge a fee for providing you with your file, unless:

1. you have requested a copy of your file within the last six months; or
2. no changes have been made to your file since the last time you received a copy.

The credit bureau must provide you with your file within ten working days of receipt of your request.

CHANGING THE DETAILS ON YOUR FILE

According to the Information Privacy Principles governing the *Privacy Act*, credit-reporting agencies must ensure that all personal information contained in your file is accurate, up to date, complete, and not misleading. Where there is any doubt about the integrity of the information in these respects, the information should be removed from the file or amended.

Credit files sometimes contain information that is inaccurate or misleading. Often, the problem stems from inaccurate information given to the bureau by a credit provider, or sloppy administrative practices inside a company. The customer relations department, for example, may not routinely inform the debt-recovery division that a debt or account is in dispute.

If, having looked at your credit file, you notice inaccuracies, request the Credit Reference Association to alter the file accordingly. To achieve this, you may need to provide some documentation.

The Privacy Act states that upon receiving a request to change information in a credit file, the credit bureau must promptly address the question of whether the amendment can be made and, if possible, accommodate the individual's request. The agency has a right under some conditions to refuse amendment.

If the CRAA says it cannot or will not change the details on your credit file, you should be notified of your right to have a statement setting out your claim included in the file. The statement should set out the details of the amendments you sought, and the background to the confusion, if any. This *must* be included in your file. If the CRAA believes the statement is too long, it must refer the statement to the Privacy Commissioner to be shortened. A statement of 150 words appears to be a reasonable length.

This being accomplished, your amended details should (under some circumstances) be sent to credit providers whom you have had contact with. The Credit Reference Association will ask you to nominate organisations to whom the amended details should be sent.

HANDLING DISPUTES ABOUT CREDIT INFORMATION

Situations often arise where credit customers dispute their terms of or record of credit. This may occur in several circumstances: for example, where you claim to have made a payment, but this is disputed by the credit provider; where there is disagreement about the amount due on each payment; in disputes about the rate of interest; or in disputes about charges.

In such cases, the law requires the credit provider and the credit reference agency to deal properly and swiftly with the dispute. If the dispute cannot be resolved, or is dealt with unsatisfactorily, the matter may be taken by the individual to the Privacy Commissioner.

DISCLOSURE OF YOUR INFORMATION

Generally, your file can be disclosed only to a credit provider, mortgage or trade insurer, another credit agency, a law-enforcement agency (in connection with a serious credit infringement), to yourself or your agent.

On each occasion that your file is disclosed, a note of the disclosure must be made on your file. This will include the date of disclosure, the inquirer to whom the information was disclosed, and, if the request related to only part of the file, information indicating the part of the file that was disclosed.

It is also important to remember that all credit providers are now required by law to notify you if they have refused you credit on the basis of information on your credit file.

The organisations which have legal access to your file are:
1. banks, building societies and credit unions;
2. retailers;
3. trade credit providers;
4. the Department of Social Security;
5. the Australian Taxation Office;
6. law-enforcement agencies in connection with the investigation of fraud or other serious credit infringements; and
7. the law courts, through a subpoena.

HOW CAN CREDIT INFORMATION BE USED?

The Privacy Act lays down very strict guidelines for the use of information contained in credit reports. The purposes it permits are:
1. to assess an application for consumer credit;
2. to assess an application for commercial credit, only when the individual has consented to such a use;

3. to assess whether to accept a person as a guarantor, where the person has consented to such a use;
4. in the case of a current credit provider, to assist the individual to avoid defaulting on a credit obligation;
5. to assist the collection of overdue payments to a credit provider;
6. to assist the internal management of the credit provider, so long as the information relates directly to the loan;
7. for a use required or authorised under law; and
8. for a use connected with a serious credit infringement where there are reasonable grounds to believe that the individual has committed such an offence.

NOTES

1. Figures supplied by Bruce Bargon, General Manager of CRAA, during an interview with the author, May 1992.
2. Senate, Questions without notice; *Hansard*, 31 May 1989.
3. *Report of the Credit Reporting Forum*, 1991.
4. Letter to the *Australian*, 7 July 1991.
5. *Law and Justice Legislation Amendment Act* 1991.
6. "CRAA and your rights to privacy" brochure, CRAA, 1992.

CHAPTER EIGHT

THE INFORMATION-EXCHANGE CLUB

"Nothing is secret which shall not be made manifest"

Luke 8:17

In 1990, the Independent Commission Against Corruption (ICAC) received evidence that employees of the New South Wales Police Department and the Roads and Traffic Authority of New South Wales (RTA) had been selling confidential personal information to private investigators. Motivated by a suspicion that the trade in personal information was widespread, ICAC commenced what was to become one of its most dramatic investigations. The decision to conduct the inquiry was set against a backdrop of rumours that many other government departments had been corruptly selling personal information for decades.[1]

Code named "Operation Tamba", the investigation uncovered massive rorts in many areas of government and the private sector. Systematic selling and swapping of personal information had become epidemic and endemic. Bureaucrats, bankers, debt collectors and police would attend parties where personal information was swapped and contacts secured. ICAC's Assistant Commissioner Adrian Roden labelled this the "Information-Exchange Club".[2]

The extent of the corruption, however, went much deeper than the occasional clandestine Christmas party. All levels of local, state and federal government, solicitors, electricity authorities, real estate agents, police, debt collectors, credit unions and the insurance industry are involved.

In its submission to ICAC, the Australian Privacy Foundation said, "While the Foundation has feared that disclosure of personal information was widespread, the extent of such practices could not have been guessed at".[3]

The New South Wales Privacy Committee, a government body, told ICAC, "Personal information provided in good faith (and frequently under legal compulsion) by the citizens of New South Wales is being bartered and sold on a breathtaking scale. Our privacy is being sold and the proceeds of the sale are lining the pockets of the corrupt."[4]

The proceeds were sometimes quite significant. One RTA employee on a base salary of $25,000 a year earned an additional $30,000 over a four-year period by selling personal files. Another employee earned $4500 from one source alone over a two-month period.[5] It was also revealed that one lower level RTA officer made more than $100,000 from three clients.[6]

The ICAC hearings provided the first opportunity to bring the issue out into the open. By having these transgressors take the witness stand, the government hoped to construct an accurate picture of the extent of the corruption.

From the first day, however, it was clear that the task was not going to be so simple. At the commencement of the inquiry, four solicitors took the stand to answer questions about their involvement in the corrupt sale of information. They had used a private inquiry agent to obtain criminal histories and, in one case, information from the RTA. An analysis of the agent's files revealed that he had obtained something like 4000 personal file checks through the RTA, and 190 criminal histories.[7]

One solicitor admitted to the commission to having asked the New South Wales fraud squad for a criminal record, and had been told that police were not authorised to give out personal details. However, when quizzed about involvement with other successful requests for personal information the solicitor told the commission that she didn't 'for one minute think ... [she] was getting someone to do something improper".[8]

Three other solicitors were also put on the witness stand. Time after time they told the commission that they truly believed that private investigators obtained their information properly and legally. In strikingly similar evidence, all four solicitors said they had never turned their mind to the question of how this sort of personal information might be obtained.

This good faith of the solicitors appears a little naive, given the sensitive nature of much of the information on police and RTA files. Police computers hold such information as motor vehicle licence details and histories, traffic convictions, motor vehicle registration information, vehicle histories, stolen and wanted vehicle information, criminal histories, warrant checks, police personnel information and crime and intelligence information. None of this information is available to members of the public, even through a Freedom of Information (FOI) request.

The RTA database includes particulars of grant, refusal, renewal, suspension and cancellation of registration and licences, the transfer of registrations, and the disqualification of people for driving any particular class of vehicle.[9]

Assistant Commissioner Roden said he was "astonished" at how solicitor after solicitor claimed to believe in the honesty and integrity of the private investigators — despite the fact that in one case, for example, a solicitor received a bill for $200 for the acquisition of the criminal histories of a man and his wife.[10]

Poor memories and claims of legal ignorance dogged the commission for the next eighteen months. Nevertheless, the quantity of information obtained by the commission was staggering. It was revealed, for example, that one private investigation firm published for its clients a list of charges for accessing certain types of information. These charges included $10 for an RTA check; $20 for a Social Security check; $20 for account details from St George Building Society; $40 for bank account details; and $50 for information from police criminal records.[11]

In one area alone (the sale of confidential information from the Department of Social Security (DSS) the following evidence emerged:

- DSS officers were involved in the infamous "Information-Exchange Club" together with banks, insurance companies, debt collectors and others. A senior police officer welcomed the guests with words to the effect of "it's us against the absconders" and "we have to all work together as a team".[12]

- DSS staff from the Liverpool and city branches have for several years been leaking files to other government departments, real estate agents and private investigators. One private investigator gave evidence that he had obtained information from the DSS which had been passed on to at least seven real estate agents, to home owners, and to a private investigator.[13]

- A credit controller with a credit union had exchanged confidentia

Credit Reference Association details for unauthorised information from DSS. The information obtained from her contacts was then sold to a debt-collection agency. The agency paid her about $2500 for this information.[14]

- A mercantile agent paid for information from the RTA, Telecom, the DSS and the Housing Commission. He was also able to obtain from a bank certain account details, including name, address and balance.[15]
- A field officer with Prospect Electricity, obtained information from the DSS, which he then passed on to several real estate agents and a private investigator. He admitted to paying for hundreds of checks over a three-year period, and said other people in his office did the same.[16]
- Several banks regularly used leaked DSS information. One bank paid an investigation firm $12,000 per month for this information.[17]

This trade in government information pales when compared to the corruption uncovered amongst New South Wales police officers. The extent of this practice and the relaxed attitude of those engaged in it is reflected in a bill sent by a private investigator to an insurance company. The bill read:

> To attend to your attorney's instructions to conduct certain inquiries in this matter, including the corrupting of several members of the Police Force, and obtaining print outs relating to the man's criminal form, then drinking with them for long periods and reporting, as attached.
> Hours: many, but say, four at $25.00 — $100.00
> Copies of print outs, compiling report, nursing hangover, mileage — nil charge[18]

The insurance company processed and paid the bill.

In the fashion of so many witnesses who preceded her, the representative of this particular insurance company appearing before the ICAC hearing had no recollection of the bill, but said she would have presumed the private investigator would be ethical, despite the choice of words in the invoice.

Serving and former police giving evidence to ICAC not only admitted to selling or giving confidential information, but also lied under oath.[19]

It was revealed at the hearings that members of a network of police in New South Wales have been using their relationships with one another and their access to records to make large amounts of money. One officer, for example, earned thousands of dollars selling Medicare information to a firm of private investigators.[20] In this case, as in others, ex-police in new occupations continue to provide information to their former colleagues.

Another detective supplied information to a former colleague, now a private investigator. Although the detective said he would only provide the information in cases involving a criminal matter, he only had the word of the private investigator to support that state of affairs.[21]

By far the greatest users of illegally obtained information are the banks and financial institutions. One particular bank paid over a million dollars over a five-year period to just one private investigator.[22] Claims by the banks that they knew nothing of the illegal practices of their private investigators were shattered when a former employee of a firm of private investigators gave evidence that her boss made a habit of discussing his practices with bank managers.[23]

The banks themselves were also directly guilty of illegal practices. The employees of one bank used a template to decipher the information on confidential government forms. In another case, to avoid detection of the bank's practices by ICAC, a senior bank executive ordered an employee to shred a contact book.[24]

The harsh light cast on the banks, police and bureaucrats by the ICAC inquiry had the effect of driving up the price of illegally obtained information but, despite the heat, the bureaucrats still offered personal information for a price. The head of a firm of private investigators told the ABC's "7.30 Report" that even during the ICAC hearing he was receiving calls from bureaucrats offering to sell personal information from their files.[25]

THE ICAC REPORT

The report of the ICAC investigation was released on 12 August 1992 and created a storm of publicity.

The report came down hard on the individuals and organisations involved in the corrupt trade in personal information: "As they have gone about their corrupt trade, commercial interest has prevailed over commercial ethics, greed has prevailed over public duty, laws and regulations designed to protect confidentiality have been ignored"[26] and, "On the basis of the evidence heard by the Commission, it would be difficult to overstate how widespread the practice has been".[27]

There was a wide spectrum of information in the trade. Addresses were obtained for the purposes of repossessing cars or delivering summonses. Criminal histories and movements in and out of the country were freely obtained. Silent telephone numbers, passport particulars, driver's licence and car registration details, bank account details and social security information were available at the right price. Correspondence going back ten years was also sold.

The report devoted only a small amount of space to the question of whether this conduct could be justified in the public interest: Assistant Commissioner Roden believed that in spite of the quest to track down debtors and defaulters, the ends could not justify the means. He pointed out that it was often not the debtor, but the debtor's family whose privacy was "grossly and gratuitously invaded". Furthermore, the justification also overlooked the fact that this corrupt trade sometimes involved quite sinister purposes, and that the bottom line of the trade is that it contributed to the corruption of public officials. [28]

The personal information disclosed usually went, first, to a private inquiry agent or a commercial agent where it was used for a "primary purpose", whether it was the tracking of a person's whereabouts, the discovery of income information, or for purposes of a similar nature. Sometimes it was then re-sold to other inquiry agents for their own purposes — usually when those agents did not have contacts in departments.

In this way, it was the public officials and the agents who were the main participants in the trade. Nevertheless, the trade would not have been possible if it was not for the direct involvement of the finance industry and lawyers, the majority of whom knew that the information they requested would have to be drawn from confidential sources.[29]

The conduct of some banks and other organisations went beyond the mere trading of information. Some organisations actively concealed their activities by using code words. Some instructed their agents to falsify reports in an attempt to hide the nature of the involvement.

Assistant Commissioner Roden described the behaviour of witnesses as deceitful and obstructive. He said the facts emerged only after breaking though a "barrier of falsehoods".[30] In the course of the hearing, 26 witnesses admitted to deliberately giving false evidence on oath. Others admitted to altering or destroying documents to obstruct or mislead the inquiry.[31] Some had met to prepare the false evidence they gave. The inquiry was riddled with lies and unbelievable stories.[32]

WHO DEALT IN THE INFORMATION TRADE?

PRIVATE INVESTIGATORS

Officers of the Roads and Traffic Authority provided ICAC with the names of several agents with whom they had dealt. Search warrants were obtained, and a considerable volume of documents were seized. All contained confidential information from the RTA. Five agents were in possession of confidential personal information from other government agencies.

Many of the private inquiry agents had cultivated contacts over many years. Most paid their suppliers by way of either a retainer of several hundred dollars a week or month, or a fixed fee for each access to the files. A single access to a criminal history might yield a ten dollar payment for the police officer, but when re-sold by the inquiry agent might fetch a hundred dollars.

Most of the agents were cautious about their dealings with public officials. One, however, had no such concerns. His payments to RTA officers was listed in his books of account under the heading "bribes".[33]

A great deal of information could not be obtained by ICAC because many mercantile agents said in evidence that they had no knowledge of the last names or addresses of the people with whom they dealt, nor could they assist the commission in locating these information suppliers. The irony was not lost on ICAC, which cast doubt on the truth of these claims.

FINANCIAL INSTITUTIONS

Throughout the inquiry, ICAC was assured by banks and other finance organisations that the trade in confidential information was not in accordance with company policy. Evidence from senior management asserted that any actions to obtain information corruptly must have taken place without the knowledge or consent of senior management. The finance industry executives, it was claimed, believed that all information was obtained legally and ethically.

The reality was far different. The ICAC report stated that the corrupt trade in information was rife. There was hardly an instance when the trade was brought to a stop when identified by management. Roden observed, "Financial and commercial institutions showed little or no willingness to let considerations of propriety, integrity, or even legality stand in the way of their commercial interest".[34]

The attitude of most management in the finance sector was one of wilful blindness. Managers who genuinely did not know of the illicit trade did not respond with concern when it was discovered. Instead, they carried on as if the facts had not emerged. There was an apparent need or desire to keep the senior management in ignorance of the tactics used. It was a case, as Roden put it, of "the boardroom wanting to remain untouched by the grime of the workroom".[35] When transgressions did come to light, the response from management was often admiration or open praise for the ingenuity of the trade.

Most of the major players in the finance industry were named by ICAC as being in some way implicated in the trade in information.

The "internal policy" of financial institutions appears often to be either imaginary, ineffective, or invisible. One finance company assured the commission that since 1988, the company had a strict policy against "illegal checks". However in evidence, the state of affairs was far different:

- An assistant to the state manager (credit control) said he knew of the checks being done up to December 1990.
- A recovery supervisor who authorised checks thought the last one had been done in January 1991.
- Another supervisor whose task was to coordinate the checks thought the last corrupt requests had been made in November 1990.

Many other officers of this particular company gave evidence that they had done or authorised checks long after the official company policy had been instituted. The same situation existed with other organisations. Between November 1990 and April 1991, management of the finance company shredded documents that they knew would be required by the ICAC inquiry. One document was shredded after a summons had been received ordering its production at a hearing.[36]

POLICE

A great volume of personal information came from police files. Much of this information related to criminal history. ICAC found that security controls in the New South Wales police department were less than reliable. Officers often used common code numbers to access the computer system, with little or no scrutiny. It was not just the police, however, who gained direct access to the criminal database. One private inquiry agent was given open access to a police station terminal to rummage at will through files. He was permitted to do this in return for bottles of liquor.

The information trade netted a good income for those police officers involved. One officer said he made up to $560 over a three-day period making illegal entries to the system on behalf of a mercantile agent.

Much of the problem can be traced to the notion police mateship. Many former police had gone into the private investigation business, and relied on the support of their former colleagues in supplying confidential information. Thirty-seven current and former police officers from constable to chief superintendent, were found to have been involved directly in the information trade.

PUBLIC OFFICIALS

ICAC discovered a disturbing confusion amongst public servants about rights of access to information, the difference between public and private information, the rights of the public and the responsibilities over maintaining security of the information.

No consistent policy has been developed in New South Wales (or in most other states) about personal information. It is quite likely, therefore, that many public servants genuinely believed that information should have been in the public domain and accessible to private investigators and others. ICAC suggested that the lack of a policy was a contributing factor in the growth of the information trade.

A culture of unofficial relationships has developed over the past few decades, leading to an acceptance of the practice by succeeding generations of public servants. Assistant Commissioner Roden observed, "Information sharing and exchange had got completely out of hand by the time this investigation had begun".[37] Nevertheless, Roden appeared to be in no doubt that the majority of the public servants involved knew that what they were doing at the time was wrong.

The second problem identified by ICAC was the lack of security in government departments and authorities. One team of RTA officers responsible for the installation of a security system was itself found to be engaged in inappropriate conduct. Elementary problems of security were found throughout the government. The entire computer tape containing entries to the police criminal history database was erased (it is thought by accident) and was therefore not available to ICAC. Rudimentary procedures were not followed. A back-up tape was not made of this important record, nor was a block placed on erasure of the tape. ICAC advised that there should be a comprehensive review of all systems in which confidential information is held.

The ICAC report recommended disciplinary action or dismissal for 33 public officials who were found to have engaged in corrupt conduct. Departments named by the commission are the Department of Social Security, the Roads and Traffic Authority of NSW, Australia Post, the Department of Immigration, the Australian Taxation Office, Medicare and electricity authorities.

OTHER GROUPS INVOLVED

Although no lawyer was found to have been involved in the corruption to the same extent as companies, Assistant Commissioner Roden expressed his concern that the trade was being supported by them. Although ICAC did not single out the legal profession, the report expressed surprise that legal professionals were involved in the first place. It would be difficult to imagine a practising solicitor ordering information that was confidential in nature without having at least a suspicion of where it was to be found.

Certain insurance and other commercial organisations were also named in the report.

In all, 250 people were identified by the investigation as being involved in the trade. The commission recommended that consideration be given to prosecution or action against 108 of these people.

The amount of money generated by the illegal trade and undisclosed to the Tax Office was considerable. Even before publication of the commission's report, the Tax Office had raised assessments worth $2,124,000 against seven people. Further assessments are pending.

The report has recommended a multi-pronged approach to the problem. First, the issue of definition must be resolved. It should be decided which information is private and which information should be made publicly available. Then, the confidential information must be made subject to strict security, while publicly available information should be easily accessible.

Any corrupt dealing with confidential information held by government should be made a criminal offence. A privacy- or data-protection law should be enacted so that the states and the Commonwealth have parallel principles of protection.

Finally, a range of laws should be amended. Private investigators should be subject to greater accountability and control; corporations engaged in corrupt information trade should be prosecuted; and the law relating to bribery should be overhauled.

Assistant Commissioner Roden was pessimistic about the trade, saying that he had no reason to assume that it was in any way significantly impaired by the ICAC proceedings. He stated, "There is no reason to believe the trade is not alive and well, if slightly wounded, today".[38]

Sale and trading of our personal information also occurs routinely outside the government and banking sectors. In one case, sales executives of a top Australian company managed to purchase the VIP address list of a leading hotel, the customer address lists of a fashionable boutique, and the executive member list of one of Australia's most exclusive clubs.[39]

The use of information of this nature extends even to political parties. The "Personal Electoral Roll System" (known affectionately as "Percy") is used by both main political parties to amass political opinions of the electorate. This information is then used for a variety of purposes, including posting out personalised messages to voters.

One federal member of Parliament admitted on ABC TV's "Four Corners" program that he entered the views of his electorate into a computer, and then sent out policy letters tailor-made to these views.[40] "Percy" can be used to collect information in ways that would be illegal under the Privacy Act: people are generally not informed that their political views will be recorded on computer.

Michael Packer, managing director of an ethical direct marketing company, CAMCO Systems, believes the unethical sale and trade of our personal information amongst companies and direct marketers is "rampant". Packer says, "In Australia we suffer from a low ethical value, where people abuse personal relationships". Packer says he has received two death threats from people in other companies because of his views.[41]

In the wake of the ICAC report, government agencies as well as Federal Parliament have set up committees and task forces to consider the findings. But Adrian Roden is cynical. Two years ago he produced a much publicised report into the bribery of officials in the course of land deals on the north coast of New South Wales. And two years later, the report is gathering dust, its recommendations largely ignored.

PERSONAL INFORMATION HELD BY THE DEPARTMENT OF SOCIAL SECURITY

Name; previous name; address; phone number; date of birth; gender; marital status, spouse; former spouse; children; country of birth; aboriginality; residence status; occupation; details of parents and other relations; applications; reviews; overpayments; prosecutions; appeals; compensation recovery; portability; information relating to ministerials/Ombudsman or parliamentary actions or correspondence; legal opinion; freedom of information details; accommodation details; personal and family financial information; property and assets information; nominee; direct credit information; social worker and welfare referral details; details of identity documents; institutionalisation and prison admission and discharge history; work history; medical details; approvals of organisations; reciprocal agreement with UK, NZ, Italy, Canada; parents' financial information and electoral roll information; physical or mental health; disabilities; racial or ethnic origin; criminal convictions; information about financial institutions and investment schemes; child support/maintenance; separation referees; taxation details; training schemes information; rehabilitation details; tax file numbers; financial information, including debts and relationship details.

Source: Privacy Commissioner, Privacy Information Digest, 1989.

PRIVATE INVESTIGATORS' CHARGES FOR SUPPLYING CONFIDENTIAL INFORMATION

Both ICAC and the Downing Street local court were presented with extraordinary inside evidence of the methods used by private investigators and the charges for obtaining illegal and confidential personal information. A brochure produced by one firm of investigators and circulated to banks and other customers provided the following costings.

No. 1 check A search of Department of Motor Transport records. This includes a registration check, driver's licence check, and engine number check. This search is carried out in all states except South Australia. Cost: $8 for NSW searches. Between $20 and $40 for interstate searches.

No. 2 check A search of Social Security records. This search will reveal whether the debtor is receiving a pension or unemployment benefits. It will give the latest address on record and the date of last payment. This search can be carried out in all states. Cost: $20 for Australia-wide services.

No. 3 check A search of Medicare records. This search will produce the last given address on Medicare files. Can be carried out in all states. Cost: $20.

No. 4 check A search of Immigration Department records. This will show whether the debtor has left the country, gives flight number and date of departure. Also shows if the debtor has arrived in the country, gives flight number and date of arrival. This search does not give a destination. Cost: $20 for all immigration searches.

Full check A full check is both no. 1 and no. 2 check. Cost: $30 (does not include an interstate transport search).

Phone number checks We are able to obtain addresses from phone numbers throughout Australia. Unable to check silent numbers. Cost: $20 for an Australia-wide search.

Post box checks We are able to obtain addresses from post box numbers throughout Australia. Cost: $20 for an Australia-wide search.

Criminal history check Gives a full criminal history of the missing debtor. Cost: $20 for search in NSW only.

NOTES

1. *Sydney Morning Herald*, 3 November 1990.
2. *Sydney Morning Herald*, 16 February 1991.
3. Submission to ICAC, 17 July, 1991.
4. Submission to ICAC, June 1991.
5. Opening remarks, transcript of ICAC's Operation Tamba hearings, 23 November 1990.
6. "Report on unauthorised release of government information", ICAC, August 1992, vol. 1, p. 5.
7. Transcript of ICAC's Operation Tamba hearings, 23 November 1990.
8. *Sydney Morning Herald*, 27 November 1990.
9. ICAC transcript, 23 November 1990.
10. *Ibid.*
11. *Sydney Morning Herald* 11 December 1990.
12. Sydney Morning Herald, 7 February 1991.
13. *Sydney Morning Herald*, 18 January 1991.
14. *Sydney Morning Herald*, 17 January 1991.
15. *Ibid.*
16. *Sydney Morning Herald*, 16 January 1991.
17. Australian Federal Police Report cited in *Sydney Morning Herald*, 29 October 1990.
18. ICAC transcript, 27 November 1990.
19. ICAC transcript of 14 January 1991 shows that a former policeman lied under oath about the receipt of money for the provision of criminal histories.
20. *Sydney Morning Herald*, 11 January 1992.
21. *Sydney Morning Herald*, 18 January 1992.
22. "Report on unauthorised release of government information", ICAC, August 1992, vol. 1, p. 24.
23. Interview with the former employee, "7.30 Report", ABC-TV, 5 December 1990.
24. "Big Brother Down Under" "Four Corners" report by Ross Coulthardt, ABC-TV 1991.
25. "7.30 Report" on ICAC findings (reporter Ian Henschke) ABC-TV, 1991.
26. "Report on unauthorised release of government information", ICAC, August 1992, vol. 1, p. 3.
27. *Ibid*, p. 4.
28. *Ibid*, p. 6.
29. *Ibid*, p. 7.
30. *Ibid*, p. 8.
31. *Ibid*, pp. 7-8.

32. *Ibid*, p. 8.
33. *Ibid*, p. 21.
34. *Ibid*, p. 135.
35. *Ibid*, p. 135.
36. "Report on unauthorised release of government information", ICAC, August 1992, vol. 3, p. 772.
37. "Report on unauthorised release of government information", ICAC, August 1992, vol. 1, p. 157.
38. *Ibid*, p. 13.
39. "Big Brother Down Under" "Four Corners" report by Ross Coulthardt, ABC-TV 1991.
40. *Ibid*.
41. "7.30 Report" on ICAC, ABC-TV 1991.

CHAPTER NINE

ENTER, THE INTELLIGENT TELEPHONE NETWORK

"I want to warn you, as the public becomes more aware that you are selling this information without their knowledge or consent, you may be heading for one of the biggest privacy showdowns we've ever had in this country. And I can tell you right now what the slogan will be — 'from Ma Bell to Big Brother'."
Marc Rotenberg, United States privacy advocate in a speech to the US telephone industry[1]

The telephone we use now is much the same device that our great-grandparents used. Its essential purpose is to send a voice message to someone who has another telephone. Slowly, other uses have become popular, such as the 0055 information lines, but the vast majority of people think of the telephone as an extension of their voice. This is all about to change.

The Australian telephone system is going through a major upgrading. Instead of the old copper cables routed through physical switching systems, the multi-billion-dollar network is changing to optical fibre and a new method of transmission called Integrated Services Digital Network (ISDN) — known more colloquially as the intelligent telephone network.

ISDN is going to mean that we will use the telephone not just as an instrument to speak through, but also as a device through which we transmit and receive a vast spectrum of information. The new system is interactive. That is, information and instructions are passed backwards and forwards down the line. By pressing numbers on your telephone at the appropriate time, you can send instructions to a receiving computer. Pressing a "1", for example, might mean "yes" to the offer of a product, while pressing a "2" could mean "charge this to my credit card". Using a series of numbers, coupled perhaps with a pin code, could give complex instructions to the building department of a local government, to an embassy for a visa application, or to a doctor for advice.

This means we can do our banking over the phone, do our shopping, or book theatre or airline tickets electronically. With ISDN technology, a computer terminal can be linked to the phone line to produce rapid and reliable two-way communications. The options for education (long distance, correspondence and "open university" education systems) are magnified magnificently. The new ISDN technology will also mean that the telecommunications companies will be able to offer a range of new services to customers. Known as Calling Line Identification (CLI), these services use a special "channel" in the signal to send your telephone number to the party you are calling. Once the called person's telephone instantly knows your number, several services are possible:

Call Return Most people have had the infuriating experience of reaching their phone just as it stops ringing? Call return is a service that "traps" the number of the caller and allows you to return the call, even if you don't know the identity of the caller.

Call Trace One of the benefits of this system is that once the identity of an incoming number is known, you can take action against harassing or obscene calls. A facility in the network will allow you to transmit the details of the telephone number to the telephone company, where it will be stored for later action (unless you receive the call from a public phone or a line which has been deliberately blocked from sending its number).

Call Screening With this facility, you can instruct the network to block a certain number of incoming numbers. If, for instance, you did not want to receive calls from a creditor, your mother-in-law, your landlord or employer, instructions could be provided via your phone, and any calls originating from those numbers would be blocked. A recorded message would advise the caller that you did not wish to receive calls "at this time".[2]

These are all beneficial services that many people would find useful. However, not all the services made possible by the new technology are to be welcomed. Australians will soon be offered a service called Call Display (in Canada and the US this facility is known as Caller

ID). Put simply, it takes note of your number and displays it on a special screen on the telephone of the person you are calling. It means that before you answer the telephone, you can see the number of the person calling you.

Sounds good? The immediate reaction of customers in North America, where this technology made its debut, was positive. People quite naturally felt they had a right to know who was calling them. Telephone companies argued that the Caller ID device was just like having a peephole in your front door. Indeed, the executive director of the Australian Telecommunications Users' Group, Wally Rothwell, recently told a seminar "I happen to take the view that if someone is knocking on my door, I should and do have the right to see who it is before I open it. I believe that right should extend to the telephone".[3]

Mr Rothwell, like the telephone companies, is portraying Caller ID as a customer-friendly, privacy-friendly service. The person receiving a call has a right to protect privacy, because the person making the call is the privacy invader. Telephone companies argue that the Caller ID issue is a control issue. They say the person receiving a call has a right to control whether or not a call should be answered. Privacy advocates also argue that Caller ID represents a control issue. They say, however, that the issue is not control over the answering of a call, but control over the disclosure of your telephone number. To reverse the onus of disclosure would create a diminution of privacy for all telephone subscribers.

The purveyors of the Caller ID service also argue that their facility will all but completely eliminate harassing, hoax and obscene calls. If malicious callers know their number will be displayed at the other end (and police can then trace the address from that number) who would take the risk? Sounds logical.

The problem is that the arguments advanced by the overseas telephone companies are deceptive and inaccurate. Obscene and threatening callers only need to use either their blocking facilities, or use a public telephone. Police departments in the US are cautious about giving unfettered praise to Caller ID. Indeed many people are angry at the police because instead of dealing with the problem of obscene callers, they often merely advise that the victim subscribe to Caller ID.

Caller ID is fraught with other problems. The greatest use of the facility will be by commercial organisations, law-enforcement agencies, government departments and direct-marketing companies. Many people who genuinely want or need to protect their anonymity will find their number published at the other end of the telephone line.

The provision of these services has caused public protests. In North America, Caller ID has become the single biggest privacy issue in memory. Some States have decided that the service has so many problems that it either should not be offered, or should be subject to severe restrictions. In California, for instance, where the State Public Utilities Commission had to decide whether to allow Caller ID, Judge Lemke bluntly concluded: "... Caller ID service would not be in the public interest, because the significant detriments associated with the feature would offset the scant benefits it offers to only a very small minority of customers".[4]

When we talk about the Caller ID facility, we have to keep in mind all the other technology that can be linked to it. Reverse directories (services that give a name and address from a telephone number) are now commercially available. In Australia, this service is called "Australia on Disk" and it provides a number-to-name match nationwide for $1500.

At the touch of a button a person or organisation receiving your call can discover not just the incoming telephone number, but also the address of that number and the name of the subscriber. The possibilities go beyond this. A whole range of information is legally available which can instantly provide a profile on you on the basis of a telephone number. You are, in fact, doing much more than communicating your telephone number to the person you call.

In an effort to demonstrate the dangers of Caller ID, a Canadian consumer affairs program "Marketplace" commissioned a private investigator, Harry Lake, to discover all he could from a telephone number displayed on a Caller ID facility. Within three hours, Lake had traced not just the subscriber's address, but also his full name and birthdate, his wife's name and birthdate, the date of purchase of his home and the price he paid, details of the mortgage and to whom it is paid, his employer and his wife's occupation, his credit cards, credit rating, vehicle details and licence plate number.[5] If Lake had had access to more sophisticated technology, these and other details would have been available far sooner than three hours.

The introduction of Caller ID in the US has been one of the main reasons why telephone companies have dropped from being the most trusted public organisations, to the fifth most trusted in a period of nine years.[6]

There can be no doubt that there is big money to be made in the service — Bell Canada made C$89 million in one year from Caller ID subscribers in Quebec and Ontario alone, and this did not include the rental of the equipment. Nevertheless, privacy advocates argue passionately that the public interest is not served by the technology. Marc Rotenberg from the public interest group Computer Professionals for Social Responsibility (CPSR) told the United States Telephone Association,

> *What is technically possible is not the same as what is good public policy. Our system of government, through the regulatory framework, is designed to ensure that citizens have some say over the technical forces that affect their lives. The protection of the environment and public safety depend on the efforts of law makers to draw boundaries around technologies that could make our world less safe, and our lives less secure. And this includes personal privacy. It is a mistake to assume that because something can be done, it should be done.*[7]

Yet telephone companies insist Caller ID is in everyone's interest. Surely no-one would mind transmitting their telephone number to the person they are calling. Surely everyone has the right to know who is calling. Surely we must do all we can to fight the plague of obscene calls in our community.

The reality of Caller ID presents a much different picture. Caller ID brings benefits to a small number of customers: namely those who only want to receive calls from a small number of fixed locations. For others, the service has bad as well as good aspects. For every advantage to customers, there are many more for the commercial operator anxious to find out a telephone number and location for direct marketing and other purposes. Not everyone wants to be bombarded with junk mail and junk telephone calls.

There are other disadvantages. The telephone companies target the benefits of Caller ID for the person receiving calls, but how about you as the caller? Think about the following scenarios.

- You are making what you think is an anonymous inquiry to the Tax Office about your late return. A few weeks later you are instructed to attend an audit.
- You make a call to find out the price of washing machines. Even though you did not volunteer your number, you start to receive telephone calls from sellers of white goods.
- You make an anonymous call to the police to report what looks like a burglary in the next house. A policeman knocks on your door that afternoon and asks that you attend the local station and produce a written statement.
- You have installed Caller ID on your phone, and told your children they are only to answer calls from two or three numbers. One day you have an accident and frantically try to speak to them from the hospital. They don't recognise the number, and consequently do not pick up the phone.
- You are listening to a current affairs program which asks you to call one of two 0055 numbers in a poll of political opinions. Suddenly you are on the mailing list of the political parties.
- You spend the morning ringing local garages to get a quote for a part. Many are engaged or the person is unavailable. Having secured the right price, you find that your afternoon is littered with unwanted calls from the garages you did not speak to.
- You make an anonymous enquiry to one company about roofing, and find that you are receiving follow-up calls every three weeks from several roofing companies.
- You accidentally dial a wrong number. The person at the other end insists you are a harassing caller and becomes angry and abusive. He has your number.
- Having had these bad experiences, you cancel your Caller ID. Now you find some people are suspicious because you have not revealed your number. Friends won't pick up the phone. Some businesses treat you like a second-class customer. The local pizza shop insists on ringing you back for verification. The school, bank, radio talkback programs and even government departments do the same.

The myth of Caller ID is that it will bring privacy and safety to telephone customers. What it will do, instead, is create new dangers. What happens to a child who has run away, or an abused wife, if they want to ring home? The short answer is that not only is Caller ID a disincentive in some circumstances to use the telephone, but to ring might be dangerous.

THE NEED FOR ANONYMITY

Many people have reason to fear the introduction of Caller ID. It is not a service that will bring joy to people who desire anonymity There are many instances where people would want to preserve their privacy and anonymity. Half a million Australians have already decided to pay for silent numbers, but listed subscribers also have reasons for opposing Caller ID. Among them would be:

- Women and children who need protection from violent estranged husbands and do not want their whereabouts known if they need for any reason to speak with either the husband or his acquaintances.
- People who work from home and make many phone calls in the course of their work, but do not necesssarily want their number identified and treated by others as a "free for all" commercial number.
- Doctors and other professionals who make calls to patients from home but who value their privacy and the time they spend with their families, and might not want clients and patients ringing back on the home number.
- Police and other law-enforcement agencies conducting investigations who would risk the secrecy of their operations if a suspect is suspicious about the incoming number. (Law-enforcement authorities in the United States have complained that drug traffickers are using Caller ID to monitor incoming calls and thus minimising the risk of a wire-tapped conversation.[8]

PRIVACY PROTECTION FOR THE TELEPHONE

There are two broad areas of traditional privacy concern that flow from Caller ID and other CLI services. One relates to personal privacy; the other, to privacy as a community-wide concern.

Telecommunications companies in other countries have successfully highlighted an apparent contradiction in the privacy argument: that of the right of privacy of the called party (the right not to have to answer unwanted calls). The distinction, however, is not challenged by privacy advocates. Only the manner of identification of the caller is challenged. If a subscriber felt a need to answer only those calls from a fixed number of people, this can best be achieved by using code names rather than numbers. A significant consumer issue arises here because identification of a caller by a number limits the mobility and options of the calling party. If you are known only by your number, you are restricted to using that number. Technical solutions may in the future be implemented to solve this dilemma, but as usual it is likely that the cost of the solution will be passed on to the consumer as a separate service.

Privacy advocates argue that the overwhelming use of Caller ID is for purposes which have nothing to do with the protection of the called person's privacy. While it is true that in a very small number of cases the interests of the called party will be genuinely served, the advocacy argument is clearly that the balance of public benefit is not served by Caller ID, and that the benefits of the service lie elsewhere (that is, with commercial uses). Advocates therefore argue that on the basis of the overall diminution of privacy, Caller ID should not be offered unless under very strict guidelines.

Perhaps the most persuasive, though most complex, privacy factor is the issue of overall diminution of privacy for society. The intelligent telephone network will generate a vastly increased amount of personal information throughout the telecommunications network and among its subscribers, and this increases the risk of privacy violation for all people. The existence of large quantities of personal information is dangerous where adequate protections are not in place.

THE AUSTEL INQUIRY

In 1991, in response to concerns about the introduction of CLI services to the Australian telephone network, the Australian telecommunications regulatory authority AUSTEL conducted an inquiry into telecommunications privacy.

The Australian Privacy Foundation's submission to the inquiry took the same position as that of privacy advocates in North America and argued:

The development of ISDN brings with it enormous advantages to telecommunications services, but also significant dangers to the violation of privacy. Caller ID appears to have limited advantage to the individual, and there is no doubt that it has the potential to create a new and far more widespread incidence of harassing and threatening calls. Direct marketers will use the proposed service exclusively for the development of marketing lists, and we believe this directly breaches the commonly held privacy principles.

It was not surprising to see the telecommunications carriers and telemarketers arguing in unison the case for unrestricted use of Caller ID. Their view generally was that all telephone numbers should be sent down the line at the time of each call unless the caller took steps immediately before the call, by entering a code, to block the sending of the number. Overseas experience indicates that many callers simply don't bother to go to the trouble of doing this. As a result, the vast majority of calls on the network are picked up by Caller ID.

There are two possible ways of dealing with the use of Caller ID. One is to allow the transmission of your number only if you make a choice before each call to do so. Otherwise, Caller ID will not become active. This is called "Opt In" or "default line blocking". Line blocking is the expression used by the carriers to mean a normal block on transmission of your number on any calls you make.

The second situation is where your number is sent down the line automatically unless you explicitly make a choice not to allow this. You do this by entering a code number before you dial the telephone number. This then blocks the transmission of your number. This is known as "Opt Out" or "default call blocking".

The United States and Canada have no single ruling on the blocking option. Each State or Province is responsible for drawing up its own guidelines. Most of North America has an Opt Out system. Much of the central and western United States has yet to make a decision on the matter, leaving the option to each individual carrier. Naturally, the carriers prefer to choose automatic transmission of Caller ID on all calls.

AUSTEL's draft report appeared to come down on the side of default line blocking. In other words, customers would have to make an explicit choice whether to send their number down the line. AUSTEL expressed concern that there would be some people in the community who could not be reached through a public education campaign, and who would thus be vulnerable to Caller ID because they would not know they could block the transmission of their number.

Although the draft AUSTEL ruling would be a good win for privacy, it is unlikely that the final decision will favour Opt In for all time. The history of caller ID throughout the world is that governments and regulatory authorities eventually capitulate to the demands of telecommunications companies and commercial users. The companies argue consistently that the Opt-In system in makes Caller ID financially unfeasible.

CONVERTING A TELEPHONE CALL INTO A PERSONAL PROFILE

Until now, the only direct-marketing issue of interest to Australians has been the avalanche of junk mail and the generation of mailing lists. With the introduction of Caller ID, a new and far more invasive form of direct marketing will be spawned.

Each time you call a company or government department which has Caller ID facilities, your number may be registered and stored on their database. This can be linked to "Australia on Disk", which provides addresses from a given telephone number. Thus, by you making one anonymous telephone call, the company or department knows who you are and — in many instances — where you live.

The organisation you called can then link this to data from the Australian Bureau of Statistics to indicate your probable financial status, family type, age and occupation. Other local government and state databases can also be instantly accessed through tapes and disks. Presto. One call, and a profile has been compiled (see page 178).

This information can be used for any number of different purposes. It can be sold to direct-marketing companies who can either send mail to you, or, more likely, make telephone calls to your home.

As if the standard telemarketing calls are not intrusive enough, tomorrow's direct marketers will have access to a new generation of technology. Automatic Calling Equipment will dial numbers from a list, and play a pre-recorded message down the line. The lists used by these machines overseas have often been generated through Caller ID registration. Some classes of this equipment will call until you answer, then pass the call to a human operator.

AUSTEL's draft report highlighted major concerns over the implications of this new technology, and urged caution in its implementation.

The debate about Caller ID is much more than a discussion about the release of telephone numbers. Privacy International explains that, for the telecommunications companies it is "a means to the end of having the public become accustomed to data being transmitted as part of telephone usage".[9]

Dr Rohan Samarajiva, a telecommunications expert from Ohio State University calls the new telecommunications environment "electronic space", and advises, "Right now, this is where the ground rules of electronic space are being defined, and the Caller ID debate, whether we like it or not, is one place where these rules are being debated in public".[10]

Samarajiva warns that if we do not take advantage of the opportuntiy for debate, the rules will be made for us. "That's the way these things go". [11]

NOTES

1. Speech to the United States Telephone Association, Washington DC, 13 September 1989.
2. This is the message used by Bell Canada for its call screening service.
3. Paper delivered at seminar on the Intelligent Telephone network organised by the Centre for International Research on Communications and Information Technology (CIRCIT), Melbourne, 1991.
4. Public Utilities Commission of California, proposed decision of A. L. J. Lemke, January 1992.
5. "Marketplace", 17 December 1991.
6. Survey cited by Rohan Samarajiva in seminar on the Intelligent Telephone network organised by the Centre for International Research on Communications and Information Technology (CIRCIT), Melbourne, 1991.
7. Speech to the United States Telephone Association, Washington DC, 13 September, 1989.
8. "Caller ID is a Hit with Maryland's Drug Dealers, "The Capital", 7 May 1990, p. A4.
9. Privacy International General Meeting, Washington DC, 17 March 1992.
10. "Marketplace", 17 December 1991.
11. *Ibid.*

CHAPTER TEN

WHAT PROTECTION DO WE HAVE?

"The harsh reality is that data protectors run the risk of being only a tiny force of irregulars equipped with pitchforks and hoes waging battle against large technocratic and bureaucratic forces equipped with lasers and nuclear weapons."

Professor David Flaherty in
"Protecting Privacy in Surveillance Societies"[1]

THE COMMONWEALTH PRIVACY ACT

In theory, at least, the safety valve against the creation of a national surveillance system rests with the Privacy Act. This piece of legislation, proclaimed in 1988, was intended to cover Federal Government agencies and departments, including Telecom (which has since then dropped out of the Act because of corporatisation).

Although the Privacy Act does not generally provide protection within the private sector (banks, commercial organisations, et cetera) the law was extended in 1991, in response to controversy over plans by the finance industry to increase the surveillance capability of credit reporting agencies. The Privacy Act now gives protection in that area.

The Privacy Act has a long and tortuous history. Its genesis can be traced to 1976, when the government of Malcolm Fraser gave the Australian Law Reform Commission a reference to look into privacy invasions at the Commonwealth level. The important three-volume report was not completed until 1983, and was presented to the new (Labor) government in December of that year.

The report included a draft Privacy Bill based loosely on a set of internationally accepted privacy principles which had been developed by the Organisation for Economic Cooperation and Development (OECD) and to which Australia was a signatory. Justice Michael Kirby, Chairman of the Australian Law Reform Commission (and now President of the New South Wales Court of Appeal) had chaired the international group that originally produced these guidelines (which were to find their way into the laws of many countries).

The passage of the proposed Bill, however, was not an easy one. First, the introduction of the Bill was delayed, partly due to the planning of the Australia Card. By the time the Privacy Bill came before Parliament in 1986 the government had decided that the Privacy Bill should be contingent on the establishment of a Data Protection Agency, but the provisions creating the Data Protection Agency were in the Australia Card Bill instead of the Privacy Bill. So, if the Australia Card Bill was opposed, the Privacy Bill could not commence. The Australia Card Bill was rejected in the Senate, and the rest is history.

The Privacy Bill that eventually emerged after the defeat of the Australia Card provided a compromise that went at least part of the way to meeting the requirements of international privacy principles. A number of strong amendments proposed by the Opposition were accepted, and the stage was set for reasonably effective privacy protection. A privacy commissioner with a respectable range of powers and a surprisingly healthy budget (now approaching $2,500,000 a year) was appointed in 1989, and a set of principles were put in place to govern personal information held in the Commonwealth domain.[2]

The principles governing the Act are set out in full at the end of this chapter but the following plain English version should serve as a more readable guide. In this overview, when I use the term "department" I mean any federal public servant or agency, as well as the credit-reporting industry.

1. A department can obtain information from you only if the intended purpose for the information is lawful. (Principle 1 of the Privacy Act)

2. A department can collect only personal information that is of direct relevance to that department's function. For example, the Health Insurance Commission is not allowed to collect details that are used to determine your pension entitlement. (Principle 1)

3. The information that a department collects has to be necessary. It is, for example, not permitted to ask you for personal details just in case the department might need them for some future purpose. (Principle 1)

4. A department cannot use unlawful or unfair means to collect information. Collecting your details through entrapment, using

threats or inducement, or asking someone else for your details is prohibited. (Principle 1)

5. When a department asks for your personal details (or as soon as possible afterwards) it must ensure that you are aware of why the information is being collected and for what purpose it will be used. The department must also tell you whether the law authorises (or demands) the collection of this information. (Principle 2)

6. A department is required to disclose to you precisely to whom (if anyone) your information will be given. If the department is aware of other people or bodies that are likely to subsequently receive your details, this information must also be given. If, for example, you provide information to the Department of Social Security, and this information is likely to end up in the hands of the Tax Office, you must be informed of this chain reaction. (Principle 2)

7. When a department collects personal details, it has the responsibility to ensure that the information is relevant to the department's purpose, as well as being accurate and up to date. (Principle 3)

8. During the collection process, a department is required to avoid intruding to an unreasonable extent on your personal affairs. Just what this means in practice is unclear. The Department of Social Security, for instance, requires information of sole parents that could be described only as offensive: sole parent beneficiaries are required on their entitlement application to answer intimate questions about their relationship with other members of the household, for example, "to what extent does [he or she] provide care, support or help to you in any of the following circumstances — (i) illness (ii) personal crisis (iii) money matters (iv) family disputes". It seems, then, that this principle is little more than an unenforceable ethical guideline for collectors. (Principle 3)

9. Once information is in the hands of a department, it must be kept secure against theft, unauthorised modification or access, or disclosure to people who have no right to see the information. (Principle 4)

10. If a department finds it necessary to give your information to someone else, it must make strenuous efforts to avoid access by

unauthorised people. In practice, this means that if a government department has the inclination to give your records to another person or agency, it must make an effort to inform the new custodian of the information about the importance of data security. It must also be very specific about who should be given access to the information. (Principle 4)

11. Any department that keeps records of our personal information must make that fact generally known. A department is required to disclose publicly not just that it keeps personal records, but also the nature and main purpose of the information (name, address, financial information, and so on), and the steps that people should take to obtain access to their records. Some agencies (e.g. those involved with national security) are exempt from giving people access to their information. (Principle 5)

12. Every department holding personal information is required to disclose the nature and purposes of the information, the classes of people on whom information is kept, the period over which the information is kept, the people who have access to the information (and under what conditions they can have access) and the steps that have to be taken by individuals to gain access to their files. This information (none of which relates to individuals) is available for public inspection, but is also given each year to the Privacy Commissioner who publishes these details in the *Personal Information Digest*, which contains details of the sort of records held in nearly 200 Commonwealth agencies and departments. (Principle 5)

13. Unless it is prohibited by law from doing so, any department holding information about you must give you access to your file. (Principle 6)

14. A department must take steps to amend a record to ensure that it is accurate, relevant, complete and not misleading. This means that if after seeing your file you notice information that is inaccurate or misleading, the department is obliged to either change it, or to make a notation that you have requested the amendment. (Principle 7)

15. If a department is not prepared, or is unable to modify your file, you have the right to request that a statement from you be included in the file. This statement would specify the information

that should have been altered, and the fact that you sought to have the file modified. Unfortunately, the Act does not require a department to advise people that they have this right. (Principle 7)

16. Before a department uses your information, it is required to make sure that it is accurate, up to date and complete. Like many other requirements of the Privacy Act, this stipulation uses the qualification "as are, in the circumstances, reasonable". This means a department would not check the accuracy of information before every use but, more likely, on a regular basis. (Principle 8)

17. A department is not permitted to use information for purposes that are not relevant to it. If, for example, the department held information about your family status, it could not use that information when dealing with your children or parents. (Principle 9)

18. If a department possesses information collected for one purpose, it is not allowed to use the data for any other purpose unless you have given consent for that other use or unless the department genuinely believes the information is necessary to lessen or prevent a threat to someone's life or health. The department can also use the information for another purpose if it is required or authorised to do so under law. (Principle 10)

19. A department is permitted to use information for other purposes if those uses are found "reasonably necessary" for law enforcement or public revenue (tax). This provision allows the mass matching of information between departments. (Principle 10)

20. A department holding information about you is not allowed to disclose that information to anyone unless either you have given consent, or you are "reasonably likely" to have known that the disclosure was likely to occur. As is often the case, this prohibition does not apply in matters where someone's health or life is at stake, where the disclosure is authorised or required under law or where tax or law enforcement require the information (Principle 11)

21. If your information is passed on to other agencies for law enforcement or taxation purposes, the department must make a note of that disclosure and place it in your file. (Principle 11)

THE PRIVACY COMMISSIONER

The first Privacy Commissioner was appointed in 1989, and will hold that post until 1994. The commissioner administers an Act of Parliament that is, at best, inadequate and, at worst, an instrument to legitimate government-endowed invasions of privacy and rights.

The Commonwealth Privacy Commissioner has five main functions:

1. To investigate any act or practice that may breach privacy law and, where the commissioner considers it appropriate to do so, to endeavour, by conciliation, to reach a settlement;
2. to promote an understanding and acceptance of the Information Privacy Principles of the Privacy Act and of the objects of those principles;
3. to prepare and to publish guidelines for the avoidance of acts or practices of an agency that might interfere with the privacy of individuals or which may otherwise have any adverse effects on the privacy of individuals;
4. to undertake educational programs and to publish an annual report; and
5. to issue guidelines and codes of practice relating to such programs as data matching within Commonwealth departments.

A glimpse into the workings of the Privacy Commissioner's office reveals a complex relationship with the Commonwealth Government. The popular view of the commissioner might be that he seeks to determine the public interest in government schemes and enforces a set of principles to control government actions. The reality is far more intricate.

The commissioner's role has been to act as a regulator, with responsibility for the establishment of privacy protection mechanisms that are not just effective, but also workable. There has been criticism of the commissioner that he has not gone as far as he could in protecting privacy.

While he appears to be comfortable with deciding the balance of public interest in relation to some areas like health, he seems less happy to do so in other areas. In evidence to a Senate committee,[3] the commissioner defined his role as being that of a technocrat, and advised "The statutory charter indicates simply that I implement the relevant privacy standards that have been agreed to by Parliament". In other words, the extent of public interest would have to be determined by ministers of the government.

The evidence given by the commissioner reveals his complex relationship with the government. Senators Rod Kemp, Sid Spindler, Amanda Vanstone and Patricia Giles each asked the commissioner for advice on the public interest aspects relating to government proposals to extend the Tax File Number system. On each occasion, however, he replied that his function was not to decide these things. He said "If I am going to retain a relationship of trust with the people with whom I deal ... I do not think I can easily cart around sets of advice and dispense them to people".[4]

THE COMMISSIONER AND THE PUBLIC

The Privacy Commissioner has considerable responsibilities for regulating the activities of Commonwealth Government departments, but is of far less direct benefit to individuals. In the year to June 1991, the commissioner's office received 170 complaints from individuals, but could assist, legally, only 66 of these people. These cases were dealt with through conciliation, and during the year 22 complaints were successfully resolved.

The following cases provide some illustration of the role of the commissioner and the sort of complaints he can handle.

A young woman wrote to the commissioner, complaining that she was denied entry to the Naval Reserve because of incorrect information given during a police check. A federal agency had provided the information, alleging that the woman was a "suspect" in relation to a criminal offence. The agency later acknowledged that the information was incorrect and apologised to the complainant. She was accepted into the Naval Reserve.

A man complained that a Federal Government department had intentionally released sensitive personal details from his file to a person outside the department. This had occurred without the complainant's consent. The department subsequently apologised, and implemented some staff training programs on the issue of privacy.

A woman complained that a federal compensation agency had used incorrect and irrelevant information in the assessment of her case. Following conciliation, the agency not only apologised, but also agreed to review the complainant's case.

Some employees of a local government authority complained about poor security over their tax file numbers. The most notable instance of lax security was when a bundle of group certificates were left openly on a desk for employees to sort through. After discussions between the commissioner and the authority, security was upgraded so that group certificates were sent out individually in sealed envelopes.

A mother and father complained to the commissioner on their daughter's behalf, claiming that her privacy had been breached because a government recruitment service had given a Federal Government agency her psychological report. The girl was allegedly refused employment because of the leaked report.[5] After conciliation, the psychiatric assessment was destroyed and the service agreed to help the girl find suitable employment.

The commissioner is able to accept any complaint relating to an alleged breach of one of the information privacy principles of the Privacy Act. It is, however, unfortunate that most individuals have no way of telling how the government uses (or misuses) their personal information.

WHY THE PRIVACY ACT IS A PAPER TIGER

The Commonwealth Privacy Act is an extremely limited law. It covers only Commonwealth Government agencies and the credit-reporting industry. It does not give protection against privacy invasion by state governments, the private sector, banking, telecommunications or the insurance industry. Nor does it cover privacy issues relating to any of the professions.

There are many advantages to having privacy legislation. There is no question that some of the more offensive activities of Commonwealth departments are reined in. Individual citizens are given some protection over the way personal files are used. However, even within its narrow scope, the Privacy Act has serious limitations. One of the most serious deficiencies is that it is not really a privacy law; it is a data-protection law. That means instead of it being concerned with the full range of privacy and surveillance issues, it deals only with the way personal data is collected, stored, used and accessed. It is not concerned, for instance, with such invasions as visual surveillance, drug testing, use of satellites or citizen denouncement campaigns.

Another problem relates to the lack of controls in the Act over the use of publicly available information (that is, information and records such as land titles and electoral rolls that are available for general public inspection). It is this sort of information that forms the basis of the LEAN system. The Privacy Act has no interest in this sort of information, and such details can thus be used in whatever way a government chooses.

Perhaps the most serious limitation of the Privacy Act is that it allows a great many privacy violations to occur in the name of law enforcement or taxation. The best known of these violations relates to the recent extensions of the Tax File Number system. Despite a government promise that the Tax File Number would remain the exclusive domain of the Tax Office, the system has been extended progressively to include such facets as unemployment benefits, pensioner benefits, family allowance, and the Higher Education Contribution Scheme. The Privacy Act or the Privacy Commissioner can do nothing to prevent such extensions. If a scheme has been established to assist law enforcement or to pursue public revenue collection and protection, the Act has only a limited application.

The Privacy Act stipulates in Principles 10 and 11 that information collected for one purpose should not be used or disclosed for any other purpose. Then the Act goes on to say that purposes related to law enforcement or revenue protection (the Tax Office) may ignore those principles. Since just about every privacy invasive government scheme is aimed at strengthening law enforcement or revenue, it makes something of a mockery of legislative privacy protection.

Perhaps the gravest limitation of the Privacy Act is that it does next to nothing to prevent or limit the collection of information. The Act merely stipulates that information has to be collected by lawful means and for a purpose "directly related to a function or activity of the collector". Thus, a virtually unlimited number of information systems can be established, without breaching the Privacy Act.

It would be a mistake to assume that law is going to solve all our privacy problems. In 1991, the Dutch privacy expert Dr Jan Holvast explained that privacy legislation "corrects the mistakes and misuses but it does not attack the way in which technology is used. On the contrary, experiences with data protection law in several countries show that these laws are legalising existing practices instead of protecting privacy."[6]

Subsequently the world-wide watchdog group Privacy International warned in its 1991 interim report to members:

Protections in law, where they exist, are sometimes ineffective and even counter-productive. Extensive information holdings by government are invariably allowed under exemptions and protections in law. The existence of statutory privacy bodies, rather than impeding such trends, sometimes legitimates intrusive information practices.

Despite the existence of privacy legislation, Australia in the early 1990s is shaping up to be one of the world's most advanced surveillance societies. There is an ingrained hostility to privacy within the bureaucracy, suspicion of it within the Australian Labor Party, and an ideological opposition to private sector privacy protection within the conservative parties.[7] People have come to believe that to oppose the government's plans is to be hostile to the best intentions of good public administration. "If you have nothing to hide, then you have nothing to fear" is a justification that we might expect from the government of a totalitarian regime rather than a liberal democracy.

The government has found a way to justify the establishment of massive computer surveillance systems. First, establish a watchdog with limited and diminishing powers; and second, infer that anyone opposing the reforms is working against the interests of the nation. By limiting the requirements of privacy law and emphasising the goals of fraud recovery, the government has successfully disabled the Privacy Commissioner. Privacy advocates are seen more often than not as extremist trouble-makers, unable to see reality. As each successive privacy invasion is established, the economic justification becomes harder to challenge.

In his 1991 Annual Report, the Privacy Commissioner warned: 'Ensuring that privacy values are respected in an age of economic rationalism is an extremely difficult task ... The claims that compete with privacy seem more significant because they are readily quantified, have an apparently undeniable objective and are said to carry no risk for the ordinary citizen ('Only rogues and cheats have anything to fear')."

Without considerable positive discrimination, a privacy commissioner can do little. Professor David Flaherty, the world's leading academic authority on privacy, has observed "The public is being lulled into a false sense of security about the protection of their privacy by their official protectors, who often lack the will and energy to resist successfully the diverse initiatives of what Jan Freese [one of Europe's first data-protection commissioners] has aptly termed the 'information athletes' in our respective societies".[8]

When the Federal Government planned to introduce its Blackbox scheme to link every pharmacist with a central computer in Canberra, invasive as the proposal was, it did not breach the Privacy Act. In evidence to the Senate Committee on Legal and Constitutional affairs, the foundation complained:

> We believe that when the Privacy Act was put through in 1988, the view of the public was that it would create a parliamentary oversight so that we never again would have a universal system of the nature of the Australia Card. What we have found is that through function creep these various systems tend to be implemented because they do not breach the Act.[9]

The foundation pointed out to the Senate committee that the public was being lulled into a false sense of security by the Privacy Act. While people expected that the Act would apply the brakes on the development of intrusive surveillance systems, the reality was that the Act condones and even assists such actions.[10] The period since the Act was proclaimed has seen an avalanche of privacy invasion in virtually every facet of government activity.

The test of privacy legislation and privacy watchdogs is whether they can limit the creation of invasive systems in the first place, rather than simply rake the embers after the systems have been established.[11] The parliamentary Opposition and the Democrats, acting virtually alone, have partially constrained the tide.

WHY THE PRIVACY COMMISSIONER IS POWERLESS TO STOP GOVERNMENT SURVEILLANCE

Although the commissioner is appointed and removed by the Governor-General, he is answerable to the Commonwealth Attorney-General, from whom his budget is drawn.

Many advocates view this lack of independence with concern. There is a view that a Privacy Commissioner should report directly to the Speaker of the Parliament, and have a budget set out independently within consolidated revenue (so that a department does not make the decision on the dollars allocated to the commissioner). In summarising the case for a Privacy commissioner for New South Wales, the New South Wales Privacy Committee had argued that "unless the Privacy and Data Protection Commissioner is completely independent of government, there is a danger that the commissioner will, in reality or popular perception, be seen to be an instrument for legitimating any privacy invasive practices and policies of government agencies".[12]

The risk inherent in all legislation is that instead of it conferring rights for people and restricting the actions of government, the law provides legal protection for intrusive government action. Such was the risk with the new privacy law. There was, from the outset, a danger that the Act and the commissioner could be used as a smoke screen. Senator Amanda Vanstone, addressing the commissioner during a 1990 Senate committee hearing warned "... there are occasions when we hear members of the Executive basically using your position, if you like, as a soother (for the development of numbering schemes etc), and saying 'Look, this is all right. The Privacy Commissioner has looked at it and he said it is OK'."[13] She later added, "The reason I am concerned about it is that sometimes people who do not necessarily have a big interest in this area (privacy) — do not know much about it — have your position waved as a magic wand of approval".[14]

The often-heard claim of government ministers than they have "consulted with" the commissioner is misleading, for the commissioner usually does not have the power to stop the government from carrying out its intentions.[15] On 1 April 1992 and again the following day, for example, Justice Minister Senator Michael Tate answered questions relating to two separate privacy concerns (and it is interesting to note the similarity of his responses). In answer to a question about the largely secret establishment of the LEAN system, he said (in part):

> It [LEAN] has been found to be quite consistent with the provisions made by the Senate so far as law enforcement activities are concerned. Indeed the Privacy Commissioner, Mr Kevin O'Connor ... has been very much involved in the development of this proposal. He has been consulted on the development of all of the privacy and security procedures that will be involved in this project.[16]

On 2 April, in answer to a question from Senator John Herron about the development of medical smart cards, Tate replied (in part): "But, of course, the Government has always in regard to these matters taken advice and put matters before the Privacy Commissioner, Mr Kevin O'Connor, in order to ensure that the sort of privacy safeguards which the Parliament and this Senate regard as so important, are indeed observed".[17]

Similar responses have been given by Senator Tate and other ministers in answer to concerns about extensions to the Tax File Number system, the re-issue of the Medicare card, and the establishment of the Pharmaceutical Benefits Scheme's Blackbox system. Whilst it is true that in each case the government did contact the commissioner, it is noteworthy that on one occasion it did so, after the event, and in others it was on the basis of "comment only". The commissioner has been able to offer his opinion, but has been invariably unable to influence the thrust of the proposals.

THE PRIVACY COMMITTEE OF NEW SOUTH WALES

The Privacy Committee of New South Wales is the pre-eminent government privacy body in Australia, and has achieved an international reputation. It has been in the forefront of numerous privacy issues, and can be relied on to provide thorough research and evaluation of privacy and surveillance issues.

The committee was established under the *Privacy Committee Act 1975*. It was a time when quite a few academics and public officials had taken the lead of overseas debate by seriously considering the privacy issue in its broadest context.

Technically, at least, the Privacy Committee is an independent statutory body with powers in both the private and government spheres. The reality is that the committee's scope has been severely limited because of a shortage of funds. The committee does not have an independent source of funds, and must compete with other sections of the Attorney-General's Department for money.

The New South Wales Privacy Committee has an excellent research and educational function, but is largely ignored by the state government. While the Attorney-General's Department — the committee's boss — spends three million dollars annually on its own information technology division, it allocates only a sixth of that amount for privacy protection for the entire state of New South Wales.[18] Requests by the Privacy Committee for a reasonable increase in staff and resources have for years been denied by the department.

The Privacy Committee is in a bizarre position. It has powers almost extensive as those of a Royal Commission, yet it cannot impose penalties in relation to any findings. It can make as many recommendations as it wishes to the government, but has no powers of enforcement.

Despite funding problems, the committee has achieved a great deal. It has developed voluntary codes with business (including credit reporting in the 1970s); it has developed privacy guidelines for AIDS, medical research, criminal-record checks, telephone information monitoring systems, employee privacy and direct marketing; and has been in the forefront of such issues as the Australia Card, Caller ID and electronic vehicle tracking.

In 1991, however, exasperated by the on-going paucity of funding and lack of encouragement from the government, the committee recommended its own abolition. In its submission to the Independent Commission Against Corruption (ICAC) on the subject of the inquiry relating to unauthorised release of government information the committee complained, "The committee has been so well controlled by budgetary constraints that the performance of its statutory functions has been seriously undermined ... the committee must line up and compete with every other branch and body funded by the [Attorney-General's] Department for a piece of the financial pie. Unfortunately for the committee, it always seems to be last in the queue".[19]

The committee recommended that a Privacy and Data Protection Commissioner be appointed to look after the privacy interests of people in New South Wales. It was a noble recommendation, as its implementation would probably mean an end to the Privacy Committee.

The committee has a good success rate in conciliating and investigating complaints relating to privacy violation. The Privacy Committee has an excellent reference library, and members of the public can use this facility by arrangement.

THE PRIVACY COMMITTEE OF SOUTH AUSTRALIA

If any one organisation testified to the ambivalence of government towards the issue of privacy, then the South Australian Privacy Committee would be the one. The committee has one full-time staff member responsible for all research, liaison and administrative duties. The committee, in addition to its privacy functions, also acts as a quasi freedom-of-information unit.

Despite funding constraints (which make the New South Wales Privacy Committee seem wealthy by comparison), the committee has performed an excellent function, particularly in the areas of liaison and education. Since 1991 the South Australian Parliament has debated a series of privacy Bills. The latest version, introduced in August 1992, would give the Privacy Committee statutory status, but would give it no powers.

The other states have no laws, no watchdogs, and appear to have very little interest in privacy protection. Queensland had a Privacy Act, but the government allowed this to expire in August 1990 because of a sunset clause (an automatic expiry provision) in the legislation. To date no replacement law has been passed by the Queensland Parliament.

The Western Australian Government proposed privacy legislation in 1991, but no funds were allocated for development and drafting of the legislation. As a result, government officers responsible for drafting the bill were forced to secure expert legal advice with little more than the offer of free coffee and biscuits. The legislation is due to be introduced into Parliament in late 1992, but is unlikely to achieve the sort of impact desired by privacy advocates.

THE AUSTRALIAN PRIVACY FOUNDATION

Beyond those relatively powerless government instruments, Australia has a number of non-government organisations that contribute to the protection of privacy. The key organisation has been the Australian Privacy Foundation, an entirely voluntary membership organisation formed in 1987 as a last ditch initiative to fight the Australia Card.

From its inception, it involved individuals from all positions on the political spectrum, and continues to do so. The foundation was instrumental in creating the final wave of opposition that eventually made the ID card politically untenable.

The foundation is Australia's only non-government privacy activist organisation. It works with civil liberties organisations and with other groups concerned with specific privacy issues and, where possible, cooperates with and supports official agencies. It is a participant in Privacy International, the world-wide privacy protection network (see page 142).

In 1988 the foundation's focus was to ensure that the government's alternative to the ID card, the Tax File Number scheme, was not an ID card in disguise, and to lobby in favour of the long-overdue enactment of national privacy legislation. A 'summit meeting' organised by the foundation in April 1988 brought Australian Taxation Office officials, politicians and privacy advocates together to examine the TFN proposals, and exposed many weaknesses in the proposals which the government subsequently rectified. The foundation also made contributions to the political debate which resulted in a greatly strengthened Privacy Bill being enacted in 1988.

In the following year, the foundation turned its attention for the first time to the private sector, and commenced a highly successful campaign against the credit industry's proposals to introduce "positive reporting", a system whereby the payment performance of every consumer debtor in Australia would be reported on a monthly basis to the Credit Reference Association, which holds files on nearly all Australian adults.

Building on the work of the New South Wales Privacy Committee and others, the foundation organised a second "summit" at which the Commonwealth ministers responsible announced that the government would legislate to ban positive reporting, and to impose comprehensive national credit-reporting laws. Later in 1989 the foundation fought a successful media and parliamentary campaign to counter the credit industry's attacks on the proposed legislation.

The APF has also enjoyed success in fighting the signing of the international tax assistance treaty and the government's proposed pharmacy Blackbox scheme. The foundation continues to fight for privacy protection, and can represent members of the public who have privacy concerns.

PRIVACY INTERNATIONAL

During 1990, leading privacy and human rights advocates from forty countries joined forces to form the World Privacy and Data Protection Network, which later became Privacy International. Until then, privacy protection at an international level had not existed, and previous attempts to form a world organisation had failed.

Although it had already been in existence for two years, Privacy International was not formally established until March 1992, when members from around the world met at its inaugural general meeting in Washington DC. Planning and policy development is now in the hands of a working group of 140 experts in 34 countries.

The organisation, a non-profit and non-partisan advocacy group, is now the premier world body in surveillance and privacy protection, and has already campaigned successfully on privacy issues in many countries.

Since its inception, Privacy International has organised campaigns in Northern Ireland, Canada, the United States, New Zealand, Thailand, the Philippines and Hungary on issues as diverse as ID cards, police activities and population-numbering systems.

The aims of Privacy International include: monitoring the nature, effectiveness and extent of measures to protect privacy and personal data; assessing the impact of new technologies on the privacy and freedom of the individual; monitoring and reporting on surveillance activities of security forces and intelligence agencies; monitoring the use of universal identification systems and mass matching of computer files; assessing the nature, extent and implications of flows of information between countries; and seeking ways through which information technology can be used in the protection of privacy.

From 1993, Privacy International will also publish an international annual report containing descriptions of privacy violations throughout the world.

OTHER PRIVACY PROTECTION

On a broader level, each state has a non-government Civil Liberties Council responsible for monitoring the full spectrum of breaches of rights and liberties. Most of these organisations are impoverished, but have traditionally been in the forefront of surveillance issues. Australians seem to accord civil rights a very low priority. At the time of writing, the last full-time non-government civil liberties worker in this country has been retrenched because of lack of funds for her salary. In contrast to the civil rights bodies in other Western nations, civil liberties organisations in Australia have very little public support. The Australian Privacy Foundation, for example, survives on less than five thousand dollars a year. Neither government nor private companies will support it. The national body, the Australian Council for Civil Liberties is supported by a handful of well-meaning lawyers.

The Victorian Council for Civil Liberties, under the presidency of Ron Castan QC, gave great prominence to privacy issues during the fight against the ID card. as did the Western Australian Council for Civil Liberties.

Consumer groups such as the Australian Consumers' Association have yet to develop comprehensive privacy policies. Other watchdog groups (the Welfare Rights Centre, the Council on Social Service, and so on) deal with issues of privacy and surveillance on an occasional basis, but have no special interest in the field.

THE AUSTRALIAN PRIVACY CHARTER

Dissatisfied with the general level of awareness of privacy problems in Australia, a diverse group of prominent lawyers, jurists, media figures, corporate representatives and community advocates independently joined forces in 1992 to find some solutions.

Thirty members of the group met in Sydney on 13 August (coincidentally, on the day following the release of the ICAC privacy report) under the chairmanship of Justice Michael Kirby. Present at the meeting were all shades of the political and ideological spectrum, including senior representatives of the telecommunications, credit reporting, medical, finance, insurance and media sectors, together with academics, consumer and privacy advocates, lawyers, computer and security experts.[20]

The meeting agreed that there has been an erosion of personal privacy in recent years and that the formation of national privacy principles would be an important measure to protect the rights of individuals. The members decided to formulate an "Australian Privacy Charter" to set out principles for use by private and public sector organisations throughout Australia.

The principles contained in the Privacy Charter will form the basis for the development of voluntary privacy protection measures within industry sectors, organisations and professions. The charter is likely to address such aspects as the collection of personal information, its storage, disclosure and use, and rights of access to information.

The group hopes that the initiative will have considerable impact on the use of personal information in Australia. The Privacy Charter Council (as it is now known) intends to construct a charter that is practical as well as memorable. As Justice Kirby remarked, "We are committed to producing a document that changes the consciousness of Australians." He added, "Having resolved to achieve these things, we are also concerned to develop a balanced solution to the problem of privacy protection — one that is acceptable to the users of information, as well as to those whose personal data is being used".[21]

The development of a "culture of privacy" in Australia — the key aim of the group — is one that is unlikely to be achieved unless the public in some way "owns" the document. The terms of reference of the Privacy Charter Council stipulate that the charter must be worded in plain English, and that it must be drawn up in consultation with the Australian community. The council is being divided into working groups to develop the draft of the charter. Privacy International will promote the charter throughout the world as a blueprint for similar initiatives in other countries.

INFORMATION PRIVACY PRINCIPLES
Principles governing the Commonwealth Privacy Act of Australia
(affecting the conduct of Federal Government agencies and the credit reporting industry)

These principles are the foundation for the way personal information should be collected, stored and used. They form the basis of legal protection of information, and set out the fundamental responsibilities of the Commonwealth Privacy Commissioner. A breach of any of these principles should be referred to the commissioner for investigation.

Principle 1
Manner and purpose of collection of personal information
1. Personal information shall not be collected by a collector for

inclusion in a record or in a generally available publication unless:
(a) the information is collected for a purpose that is a lawful purpose directly related to a function or activity of the collector; and
(b) the collection of the information is necessary for or directly related to that purpose.
2. Personal information shall not be collected by a collector by unlawful or unfair means.

Principle 2
Solicitation of personal information from individual concerned
Where:
(a) a collector collects personal information for inclusion in a record or in a generally available publication; and
(b) the information is solicited by the collector from the individual concerned;
the collector shall take such steps (if any) as are, in the circumstances, reasonable to ensure that, before the information is collected or, if that is not practicable, as soon as practicable after the information is collected, the individual concerned is generally aware of:
(c) the purpose for which the information is being collected;
(d) if the collection of the information is authorised or required by or under law, the fact that the collection of the information is so authorised or required; and
(e) any person to whom, or any body or agency to which, it is the collector's usual practice to disclose personal information of the kind so collected, and (if known by the collector) any person to whom, or any body or agency to which, it is the usual practice of that first-mentioned person, body or agency to pass on that information.

Principle 3
Solicitation of personal information generally
Where:
(a) a collector collects personal information for inclusion in a record or in a generally available publication; and

(b) the information is solicited by the collector;

the collector shall take such steps (if any) as are, in the circumstances, reasonable to ensure that, having regard to the purpose for which the information is collected:

(c) the information collected is relevant to that purpose and is up to date and complete; and

(d) the collection of the information does not intrude to an unreasonable extent upon the personal affairs of the individual concerned.

Principle 4
Storage and security of personal information

A record-keeper who has possession or control of a record that contains personal information shall ensure:

(a) that the record is protected, by such security safeguards as it is reasonable in the circumstances to take, against loss, against unauthorised access, use, modification or disclosure, and against other misuse; and

(b) that if it is necessary for the record to be given to a person in connection with the provision of a service to the record-keeper, everything reasonably within the power of the record-keeper is done to prevent unauthorised use or disclosure of information contained in the record.

Principle 5
Information relating to records kept by record-keeper

1. A record-keeper who has possession or control of records that contain personal information shall, subject to clause 2 of this Principle, take such steps as are, in the circumstances, reasonable to enable any person to ascertain:

(a) whether the record-keeper has possession or control of any records that contain personal information; and

(b) if the record-keeper has possession or control of a record that contains such information:

   (i)   the nature of that information;

   (ii) the main purposes for which that information is used; and

   (iii) the steps that the person should take if the person wishes to obtain access to the record.

2. A record-keeper is not required under clause 1 of this Principle to give a person information if the record-keeper is required or authorised to refuse to give that information to the person under the applicable provisions of any law of the Commonwealth that provides for access by persons to documents.

3. A record-keeper shall maintain a record setting out:

(a) the nature of the records of personal information kept by or on behalf of the record-keeper;

(b) the purpose for which each type of record is kept;

(c) the classes of individuals about whom records are kept;

(d) the period for which each type of record is kept;

(e) the persons who are entitled to have access to personal information contained in the records and the conditions under which they are entitled to have that access; and

(f) the steps that should be taken by persons wishing to obtain access to that information.

4. A record-keeper shall:

(a) make the record maintained under clause 3 of this Principle available for inspection by members of the public; and

(b) give the commissioner, in the month of June in each year, a copy of the record so maintained.

Principle 6
Access to records containing personal information

Where a record-keeper has possession or control of a record that contains personal information, the individual concerned shall be entitled to have access to that record, except to the extent that the record-keeper is required or authorised to refuse to provide the individual with access to that record under the applicable provisions of any law of the Commonwealth that provides for access by persons to documents.

Principle 7
Alteration of records containing personal information

1. A record-keeper who has possession or control of a record that contains personal information shall take such steps (if any), by way of making appropriate corrections, deletions and

additions as are, in the circumstances, reasonable to ensure that the record:

(a) is accurate; and

(b) is, having regard to the purpose for which the information was collected or is to be used and to any purpose that is directly related to that purpose, relevant, up to date, complete and not misleading.

2. The obligation imposed on a record-keeper by clause 1 is subject to any applicable limitation in a law of the Commonwealth that provides a right to require the correction or amendment of documents.

3. Where:

(a) the record-keeper of a record containing personal information is not willing to amend that record, by making a correction, deletion or addition, in accordance with a request by the individual concerned; and

(b) no decision or recommendation to the effect that the record should be amended wholly or partly in accordance with that request has been made under the applicable provisions of a law of the Commonwealth; the record-keeper shall, if so requested by the individual concerned, take such steps (if any) as are reasonable in the circumstances to attach to the record any statement provided by that individual of the correction, deletion or addition sought.

Principle 8
Record-keeper to check accuracy etc. of personal information before use

A record-keeper who has possession or control of a record that contains personal information shall not use that information without taking such steps (if any) as are, in the circumstances, reasonable to ensure that, having regard to the purpose for which the information is proposed to be used, the information is accurate, up to date and complete.

Principle 9
Personal information to be used only for relevant purposes

A record-keeper who has possession or control of a record that contains personal information shall not use the information except for a purpose to which the information is relevant.

Principle 10
Limits on use of personal information

1. A record-keeper who has possession or control of a record that contains personal information that was obtained for a particular purpose shall not use the information for any other purpose unless:

(a) the individual concerned has consented to use of the information for that other purpose;

(b) the record-keeper believes on reasonable grounds that use of the information for that other purpose is necessary to prevent or lessen a serious and imminent threat to the life or health of the individual concerned or another person;

(c) use of the information for that other purpose is required or authorised by or under law;

(d) use of the information for that other purpose is reasonably necessary for enforcement of the criminal law or of a law imposing a pecuniary penalty, or for the protection of the public revenue; or

(e) the purpose for which the information is used is directly related to the purpose for which the information was obtained.

2. Where personal information is used for enforcement of the criminal law or of a law imposing a pecuniary penalty, or for the protection of the public revenue, the record-keeper shall include in the record containing that information a note of that use.

Principle 11
Limits on disclosure of personal information

1. A record-keeper who has possession or control of a record that contains personal information shall not disclose the information to a person, body or agency (other than the individual concerned) unless:

(a) the individual concerned is reasonably likely to have been aware, or made aware under Principle 2, that information of that kind is usually passed to that person, body or agency;

(b) the individual concerned has consented to the disclosure;

(c) the record-keeper believes on reasonable grounds that the disclosure is necessary to prevent or lessen a serious and imminent threat to the life or health of the individual concerned or of another person;

(d) the disclosure is required or authorised by or under law; or

(e) the disclosure is reasonably necessary for the enforcement of the criminal law or of a law imposing a pecuniary penalty, or for the protection of the public revenue.

2. Where personal information is disclosed for the purposes of enforcement of the criminal law or of a law imposing a pecuniary penalty, or for the purpose of the protection of the public revenue, the record-keeper shall include in the record containing that information a note of the disclosure.

3. A person, body or agency to whom personal information is disclosed under clause 1 of this Principle shall not use or disclose the information for a purpose other than the purpose for which the information was given to the person, body or agency.

NOTES

1. D. Flaherty, *Protecting Privacy in Surveillance Societies*, University o North Carolina Press, Chapel Hill, 1989, p. 393.
2. Roger Clarke, "The resistible rise of the national personal data system" *Software Law Journal*, vol. v, no. 1, February 1992.
3. Standing Committee on Legal and Constitutional Affairs (Senate) *Hansard*, 19 October 1990.
4. *Ibid.*
5. Privacy Commissioner, *Annual reports* 1990, 1991.
6. Jan Holvast, "Vulnerability of information society", in *Managing Information Technology's Organisational Impact*, Clarke, R., and Cameron J., (eds), North Holland Amsterdam, 1991.
7. This does not apply where privacy invasions arise from governmen initiatives, though the conservative parties are slow to react even to these threats.
8. D. Flaherty, *ibid.*, p. 385.
9. Standing Committee on Legal and Constitutional Affairs (Senate) *Hansard*, 17 June 1991.
10. Roger Clarke, *ibid.*
11. James Rule, *The politics of Privacy*, Mentor, New York, 1980.

12. New South Wales Privacy Committee, submission to the Independent Commission Against Corruption, June 1991, p. 30.

13. Standing Committee on Legal and Constitutional Affairs (Senate), *Hansard*, 19 October 1990.

14. *Ibid.*

15. Roger Clark, *ibid*, p. 58.

16. Senate, *Hansard*, 1 April 1992.

17. Senate, *Hansard*, 2 April 1992.

18. Attorney-General's Department, *Annual Report*, 1991.

19. Privacy Committee of New South Wales submission to ICAC, 1992.

20. The meeting took place at the Law School of the University of New South Wales, which hosted the Charter Group.

21. *Age*, 17 August 1992.

CHAPTER ELEVEN

WHAT THE FUTURE HOLDS

"The death of democracy is not likely to be assassination from ambush. It will be a slow extinction from apathy, indifference and undernourishment."

Robert Maynard Hutchins

To this point in *Big Brother*, I have explored the impact of information technology on a variety of aspects in our society and lives, and have attempted, piece by piece, to construct something resembling an equation so that each segment of the jigsaw can be better understood. Caller ID, government surveillance, computer matching, identity cards, common numbering systems, law enforcement, satellite tracking, credit reporting, direct marketing, denouncement campaigns and smart cards all play a part in this frightening equation.

While it will be clear that the Commonwealth Government holds massive amounts of information about each of us, we should remember that it is not the only one: state governments and their agencies; private sector organisations, such as banks and insurance agencies; as well as intelligence and law enforcement organisations hold files on the majority of Australians.

The Australian Federal Police, for instance, has a database called Internal Minutes/Reports. It contains information about the physical and mental health, sexual life, financial affairs, racial and ethnic origin, criminal convictions, religious and political beliefs, Tax File Numbers, relationship details and criminal intelligence of over ten million Australians. It is just one of more than two hundred databases operated by the Australian Federal Police, containing in total an estimated seventy million files.[1] We still do not know enough about what sort of information is collected, nor how it is used. It is clear from the ICAC investigation that all kinds of personal data about individuals flows through to areas which should not have access to it.

Most important of all, we are facing the emergence of technologies that are going to affect Australia in future years. There are many categories of these innovations. The issues that are perhaps of greatest significance are the development and implementation of DNA and genetic coding technology, the intelligent communication network, "smart" ID cards linked to the biological identity of the holder, and the establishment throughout the world of computer compatibility, allowing all computers to speak with one another.[2] Obviously these technologies may bring some benefits to human-kind, but they may also become a permanent curse.

Knowledge of this growing surveillance web leaves most people feeling dazed and powerless. Such a reaction is well and truly justified. The harsh reality is that nothing of substance exists to protect us from the web. The media have difficulty coming to grips with the issues. Our politicians seek simple solutions to extract more revenue. Government regulatory agencies such as the Privacy Commissioner and the banking ombudsman are unable to put a stop to the construction of the web. Law often gives the intruders a licence to proceed with their plans by permitting surveillance schemes instead of restricting them. Australia's advocacy groups and civil liberties organisations are so impoverished that many can hardly afford to pay their phone bills, let alone hire staff to raise public awareness and run campaigns. Meanwhile, the bureaucrats increasingly act within the scope of administrative regulations rather than under the direct authority of law. They succeed, therefore, in escaping the restraint of public accountability and scrutiny.

Just who is accountable for these invasions should be a matter of serious and ongoing debate. Instead, the issue has been discussed just once, for a mere one and a half minutes, by a Parliamentary committee inquiry. The view expressed by the witness, the Australian Privacy Foundation, was that the buck stopped with Parliament, and that parliamentarians, as representatives of the people, should be obsessed with the issue of civil rights and surveillance.

Given the depressing mass of evidence about the growing surveillance web, we have every right to feel very concerned. The surveillance question has become so complex that few people understand even a small part of the issue. At the time of writing there are no fewer than 120 key privacy issues, so it is not surprising that neither parliament nor the media are inclined to deal with the subject in any depth.

I do not know how we are going to come to grips with the emotive argument advanced by the government about the desirability of catching cheats and criminals. Obviously it would be a valuable exercise indeed to weed out every crook safely and easily. The answer to social problems, however, is not necessarily tighter and more authoritarian government. The more tightly controlled a population becomes, the greater will be the incidence of victimisation. The authoritarian system itself will ultimately become the justification for ever more rigid controls.

The government's cost benefit justifications are, as I have discussed throughout this book, based in many instances on flimsy figures and creative calculations. The Auditor-General has already determined that this is the case.[3] Still, even if the various surveillance systems could bring the promised returns, the money would hardly justify the sad outcome for Australia's liberty.

HOW MUCH MONEY WILL THE ULTIMATE SURVEILLANCE WEB GIVE US?

If we allow government to introduce all the surveillance schemes that are technologically possible, what sort of fiscal gains might we expect? How much can we expect to add to the public purse if we mass match every computer file in Australia, give government ongoing access to our bank accounts, create a high-integrity identification and common numbering system, and manacle the population to the surveillance web?

My (possibly) very flimsy speculation is that, taking into account the savings currently achieved through fraud reduction exercises, the governments — state and federal — could possibly recover a net amount of four billion dollars per year using the ultimate surveillance web. A similar amount might be recovered by the private sector, mainly by banks and insurance companies, making a total of eight billion dollars. Much of this money would be recovered from people currently using the cash economy to earn tax-free income through part-time or occasional jobs.

This calculation is speculative because no-one knows exactly how much money is defrauded from the government and the private sector each year. Estimates range to thirty billion dollars. I have taken a simple mid-point estimate, and deducted two costs: the first is the massive infrastructure cost (say, three billion dollars) of the surveillance web — computers, staff, and so on (at least proportionately equivalent to the Australia Card proposal but on a much larger scale)[4]; the second is a ballpark estimate of the alternative fraud schemes that would, as always, be developed in the wake of such government's efforts (say, four billion dollars).

Before making an attempt to calculate the cost benefits of the impending surveillance web, we should spend a moment looking at the cost-recovery basis for schemes such as data matching. Take just one brief look at the ministerial speeches relating to these schemes, and it becomes clear that there is a great deal of double counting involved. Savings from government schemes, for example data matching, are carried over from year to year. The savings from a hundred people caught out in 1992 will be carried over three, four or even five years and included in the estimates for those years So, if 1000 people are caught out by data matching each year to 1997, the 1998 figures will allege savings related to 6000 people. Bureaucrats and politicians alike appear to be recycling the same incidences of fraud to justify many different systems. This may well have been a key reason why the Tax File Number scheme blew out by 750 million dollars (a fact which the media almost universally failed to investigate).

In addition to the sin of double counting, bureaucrats fail in many instances to consider the law of diminishing returns. It is a law of commerce which says that attempts to improve efficiency, diminish fraud, increase productivity, or streamline internal administration get tougher as you progress. The first stages of an initiative usually reap the easiest and highest returns. Thus we can expect fewer returns for each successive privacy invasion, until the point comes where there will be a negative cost factor (as there was with the proposed Blackbox pharmacy computer scheme).

On the basis of current experience, we might expect to uncover about half to three-quarters of the existing fraud. However, in doing so, we would also create new opportunities for fraud. The construction of a vast electronic financial web would bring with it a wide spectrum of opportunities for computer crime. Cash — untraceable and anonymous — would increasingly be used as an alternative economy.

Even if the government was to extend the provisions of the *Cash Transactions Reporting Act* to make cash difficult to use in the retail sector, some black money would still exist. To succeed in eliminating most tax evasion and fraud, cash would be outlawed (or subject to a tax or penalty) for transactions over, say, a thousand dollars, so people would be forced to use some form of electronic card.

The only solution — the final solution — would be a nationally issued smart ID card containing our biological code. The owner of a card would be the only person in the world (at least in theory) who could operate the card, and every transaction would be monitored by the government. The card would also track geographic movements, and so if the owner offended, apprehension would be swift. Such a card is currently in production in Malaysia for international distribution (see Chapter Four).

The eight billion dollars government and the private sector might recover sounds like a great deal of money. It probably is — but not compared with the loss of freedom for our society and the virtual destruction of individual rights and privacy. Eight billion dollars is about $480 per year for every Australian.

So, based on these calculations, the difference between Australia as a relatively free society and Australia as an authoritarian Zone 5 surveillance state is about ten dollars a week for each of us.

WHAT CAN WE EXPECT FROM OUR GOVERNMENT?

When Neal Blewett was the minister responsible for the Australia Card, he strenuously defended the government's right to limit individual rights in the public interest.[5] Five years later, when the Federal Police handed the Department of Social Security details of demonstrators arrested at the 1992 AIDEX Defence Expo, the department then investigated the personal affairs of those arrested. Neal Blewett handed out a press release stating that he was "fully satisfied" and claimed that "taxpayers expect nothing less" than such an action.[6]

One of the key questions relevant to the struggle to understand the surveillance society is simply: "Who is driving it?" Bureaucrats, politicians, or both?

Public servants have a very important role to play in the

development of the surveillance state, and they are regularly blamed for such initiatives as the Australia Card and data matching. They do not, however, hold all the cards. Although politicians rely constantly on departmental staff to develop policy, there is a very clear chain of command. If the political will exists, the bureaucrats will change direction.

Both politicians and bureaucrats have relied on confusion and patriotism amongst the public to allow these schemes to prosper. Once, however, the electorate starts to seriously question the validity of surveillance mechanisms, the political parties are likely, ultimately, to respond. A parliamentary inquiry into fraud in 1992 was told, "We need to think beyond the traditional arguments used to justify mechanisms for efficiency and fraud control. In other words, it is no longer safe or appropriate to accept on face value the Government's simple intention to catch cheats and criminals".[7]

For this questioning to begin, we have to clarify precisely what mechanisms should be scrutinised. We need to identify the surveillance web as being an adjunct to government administration. Surveillance machinery is not necessary for good government; it can be a useful parasite, but not all parasitical relationships are beneficial to the host.

To keep abreast of the government's strategies, and to become empowered to do something about them, Australians ultimately will have to stop viewing government administration as one unchangeable integrated mechanism, and instead take the view that each of its parts can be examined and judged in isolation. We do this regularly with revenue and benefits issues (for example the Fringe Benefits Tax, Goods and Services Tax, Higher Education Contribution Scheme, and so on) so there is no reason why we should not scrutinise the government's internal mechanisms.

If the bureaucrats are given a free hand to construct surveillance machinery, they will often do so without fully considering the implication to aspects of freedom or liberty. One of the disturbing trends in Canberra is the way the establishment of these technological mechanisms seems to have become a virtual requirement within the jurisdiction of Senior Executive Service members.[8] Technological advances in the bureaucrats' domain count as important components of their social, political and career environment. It goes without saying that any measure to increase revenue or reduce cost is a necessary coup for these people.[9] And, of course, is perceived as beneficial unfortunately the function creep syndrome tends to swing into action whenever technology is utilised. A second commissioner of the Australian Tax Office, Michael Carmody, says, "The biggest problem [with technology] is the new opportunities which become apparent ... Having the tool can open up your mind to doing different things".[10]

The way the bureaucratic system works highlights the essential privacy problem so often identified in the preceding chapters. Modern technology, bringing power and prestige to those who use it, can be a dangerous weapon in the hands of the shortsighted and arrogant The technology is no more neutral than an atom bomb. The people who have been entrusted to manipulate the technology have a responsibility to ensure that it is used for the benefit of humankind It so often seems the case that technologists and bureaucrats do not fully take into account reasoned and intelligent consideration of the impact of their innovations.

The private sector (banks, insurance companies and the like) should not be exempted from this criticism. They have been responsible for some of the worst intrusions into the rights of the individual. Free marketeers base their reckoning of social justice on the equation that if it's good for competition, then it's good for the stock holders, and therefore good for society. That reasoning has changed little in two centuries

It's tempting to excuse the private sector as a fairly harmless player compared to the government. This might have been true (at least to an extent) a decade ago, but not so these days. The insurance industry is demanding a greater volume of personal information in return, they say, for more competitive premiums. Each year sees insurance companies establish closer links with such government agencies as the Federal Police and the Tax Office. The finance sector has become a virtual arm of government since nearly all our information held in banks and other institutions is passed routinely onto government. This working relationship between public and private sector will grow in importance over the next two decades to the point where all personal information may ultimately be subjected to government scrutiny and control.

The ultimate privacy nightmare is the development of a Zone state of surveillance. In such a scenario, public and private sector organisations, facing common enemies, end up with indistinguishable databases. The public, browbeaten by horror stories of subversives and criminals, capitulates to the surveillance mentality.

The last nail in the surveillance coffin is the fusion of the biological and the technological. When our masters decide that biological identification will be mandatory to operate the wonderful technology that exists in society, the surveillance web will be complete. Human and machine will be as one. Every individual that interacts with the information infrastructure will be personally known to that machinery. That technology exists right at this minute. Whether it is implemented will depend on how willing the population is to prove their innocence at every turn.

WHERE DO WE GO FROM HERE?

First, we have to call a spade a spade. Australian National University Associate Professor Roger Clarke says bluntly that the machinery being established is "an orchestrated campaign by senior bureaucrats to bring the Australian public to heel".[11]

There is no doubt that the government and the bureaucracy have acted with arrogance in setting up the surveillance web. I know of only three Labor Members of Parliament and seven coalition MPs who have taken any serious interest in what is happening. The Democrats have had a long and involved interest in surveillance proposals, and in many cases have gone at least part of the way to limiting their immediate impact. The problem, however, is that the systems develop a life of their own once they are in place.

In order to take action to change any entrenched policy of public administration, we need two commodities: facts and fury. Every concerned Australian should demand that elected representatives closely scrutinise what is happening, and report back to the electorate. If enough elected members — especially back benchers — raise the issue in the party room, the environment of support and compliance will soon vanish.

Perhaps the most direct and effective solution, however, is to support the organisations which have pledged to oppose the surveillance structure. The councils for civil liberties are crying out for active members. The Australian Privacy Charter, in order to succeed, needs people to commit their support. I personally am

committed to the Australian Privacy Foundation, not just because
of my association with that organisation, but because it has the run:
on the board.

The Privacy Foundation can make a ferocious impact when it ha:
the public support — the campaign against the ID card proved that
It can engineer the establishment of powerful legislation if it has the
resources — the victory to establish credit reporting laws proves that
Right now, the Foundation needs to appoint full-time staff to
investigate the government's proposals, mount high profile campaigns
initiate effective political lobbying tactics, and tell the Australian people
exactly what is happening behind the scenes.

IS THERE ANY HOPE?

As the ink dries on this chapter, the Europeans have launched a satellite
that has the capacity to identify every animal and every plant on every
farm of the continent with the aim of reducing farm subsidy fraud.[1:
The 'eyes' of Big Brother are very definitely upon us. People keep
telling me that my warnings are too little, too late. I am told by well
meaning colleagues that the surveillance mechanisms are now in place
and cannot be removed. Organisations, I am assured, have made
massive investments in information holdings, and they will no
dismantle them.

I agree with these views only to a point. The awareness of privacy
invasion is at the same level now that the environmental movemen
was twenty years ago. Back then, the Greenies were assured that their
quest was fruitless. They were told: industry serves a legitimate
function; there has to be a cost; the polluters are not going to budge
and, in any case, nothing can be done. Like the modern privacy
advocate, the environmental activist in the 1960s and 1970s was
viewed widely as a ratbag who worked against the interests of society.

At the beginning of this book I warned that Australia is witnessing
its last years as a free society. Nevertheless, gloomy as I am, I believe
that we can fight successfully to regain lost liberties, and to put in
place powerful and meaningful safeguards so that future generations
will never have to experience that horrible feeling of dazed powerlesnes:
that so many of us are experiencing now. All we need is a belie:
that we are at least as powerful as the technology we have created.

NOTES

1. Privacy Commissioner, *Personal Information Digest*, 1990. Estimates are based on calculations of separate reports in the *Digest*, and are not the Commissioner's.
2. This harmonisation, known as Open Systems was adopted formally by the Australian Government in 1991.
3. Assessment of the proposed PBS computer linkage, 1991.
4. This was estimated, in 1987 figures, variously at between 500 million and one billion dollars, with an ongoing infrastructure budget.
5. *West Australian*, 10 June 1986.
6. Press release from the office of Neal Blewett, Minister for Social Security, 17 February 1992. The Privacy Commissioner ruled in June 1992 that the handing over of the information breached the *Commonwealth Privacy Act*.
7. House of Representatives Committee on Banking, Finance and Public Administration, Inquiry into Fraud on the Commonwealth, 17 July 1992. Evidence of the Australian Privacy Foundation.
8. Top ranking public servants are represented by a special organisation called the Senior Executive Service.
9. For an assessment from a political science perspective of this issue, read Colin Bennett, *Regulating Privacy*, Cornell University Press, New York, 1992.
10. Quoted in Timothy Dixon, *The cart before the horse? The impact of information technology on taxation and social security policy*, unpublished Honours thesis, Department of Government and Public Administration, Sydney University, 1991, pp. 96, 97.
11. "7.30 Report" on the LEAN system, ABC-TV, 1991
12. "Spies in the sky zero in on farm cheats", *The European*, 23-26 July 1992, p. 1.

GLOSSARY

Anti-viral software computer software that searches through files and disks to discover viruses. Once such a virus has been detected, the virus buster can either alert the user or excise the virus without damaging the other files. These virus detectors can also keep a watching brief on a system and alert the user if a suspicious entry is being made.

Australia Card a discredited proposal of the Hawke Government to provide Australians with a high-integrity multi-purpose national identity card. The card would have been used to establish entitlement to a range of benefits and to participate in mainstream society. The plan was dropped in 1987 in the wake of massive protests.

Australian Privacy Foundation (APF) Australia's first non government privacy watchdog. The APF organised the successful campaign against the Australia Card.

Automatic calling equipment the generic name for telemarketing machines that automatically dial and process calls. These machines have a range of functions, but the most notorious of them have an automatic recorded message promoting a product or service. The machine runs off a set of numbers generated from telemarketing lists.

Automatic Teller Machine (ATM) Australians have embraced these machines in a way that bankers in other countries could scarcely dream of. It is not unusual to find a queue of people wanting to use an ATM, while the bank remains virtually devoid of customers. Many ATMs now incorporate camera surveillance.

Back-up copies made of a file held on a workstation or personal computer. Back-ups are made in case of hardware failure, file damage or accidental erasure.

Big Brother term invented by author George Orwell to describe the governing machinery of a future nightmare society. The term is occasionally mutated more accurately in the modern context to Big Family.

Biometric identification any identification procedure that relies on analysis of a physical characteristic, for example, retina, fingerprint, DNA, lip-print.

Bit a single basic unit or piece of information. Short for "Binary Digit". Eight bits of information make a **byte**, which makes a single character.

Blackbox the computer device which was planned in 1991 by the Australian Government to be installed in every pharmacy and linked to a central database in Canberra. The Blackbox scheme was proposed as a pharmaceutical eligibility checking system, but was dropped when the cost-benefit estimates were found to be false.

Bugs an error in a computer program that causes a malfunction. The term derives from a joke told in a computer lab in the 1940s when a lab worker found a dead insect in a computer print-out.

Byte an 8-bit binary code. Bytes can be used for storing any information.

Call Blocking a facility which allows telephone callers to stop the transmission of their number to the receiving party telephone. The blocking code is entered before each call, otherwise the calling number's identification is sent to the called party, where it may show on a Call Display device.

Call Display see **Caller ID**.

Call Return a telecommunications facility that automatically records the number of an incoming call so that the number can be called back at the convenience of the receiving party.

Call Screen A facility that allows a telephone subscriber to automatically block the receipt of certain telephone numbers (usually up to 12). Callers from these numbers would receive a recorded message that the called party did not wish to receive the call.

Call Trace a telecommunications facility that allows a person receiving a harrassing or obscene telephone call to have the calling number automatically registered in the telephone company's database.

Caller ID or **Call Display** a facility provided by a telephone company, which displays the number of an incoming caller. It should more correctly be known as "calling line identification" as it identifies the calling number rather than the caller.

Cash Transactions Reporting Agency (CTRA) a Federal Government agency which has the responsibility for monitoring the movement of cash through the financial system. The information obtained by the CTRA arises from mandatory reporting by financial institutions of flows of cash (of $10,000 and above by law, but in practice usually above $5000).

Compact Disk: Read Only Memory (CD ROM) a computer-readable disk that is capable of storing vast quantities of information

Computer crime a crime committed against a computer using a computer or by using the communications media between computers. Includes larceny (hardware equipment theft), electronic data interchange fraud, electronic funds transfer fraud, network phantoms, viruses, voice-mail terrorism and fax graffiti.

Computer matching see **Data matching**.

Cracker a person who illegally enters computers. Not to be confused with **hacker**.

Credit agencies private organisations that hold information on the credit histories of people who have come into contact with finance, banking or other organisations. In Australia the key credit reporting organisation is the Credit Reference Association of Australia (CRAA) which holds files on nearly 10 million people.

Crimoid the sort of computer crime created or nurtured by intense media reporting in aspects of computer crime. Examples include privacy violations, **phone phreaking**, electronic letter bombs, **hacking**, software piracy, **Trojan horses**, fax graffiti and communications eavesdropping.

Cryptography the making and breaking of secret codes. As with codes used in military exercises, the aim is to give messages the appearance of random gibberish. These codes can be broken by any computer user with the right software key.

Cyberpunks a term coined in science fiction novels of the mid-1970s to describe computer users whose nervous systems could be electronically linked to the world's computer networks (a process known as "jacking in"). The term is sometimes used to describe young hackers living "on the **network**".

Cyberspace a term devised by the author of *Neuromancer*, William Gibson, for the sum total of all computer memories and databases linked together by the world-wide computer network. In more recent use, the term implies a way of looking at and living in the universe.

Data matching a process whereby information on one computer is mass matched against parallel information on another computer. The best known example is the data-matching process between the Australian Taxation Office and the Department of Social Security.

Data protection a legal term sometimes confused with privacy. Data protection is the set of rules governing the collection, handling, use, disclosure and access to files containing personal information. Data protection is only one aspect of privacy.

Direct marketing the practice of matching individual characteristics and purchasing potential with available products and services. Direct marketers, traditionally, are the natural enemy of privacy advocates because they often breach many of the fundamental privacy principles; for example, that personal information should not be used for purposes other than those for which it was originally intended.

Disk a computer storage mechanism consisting of a rotating or rotatable plastic disk covered with a magnetic layer upon which data can be written and stored. Data can be accessed by reading heads. A hard disk spins continuously to reduce the access time to fractions of a second. Most personal computers have both forms of disk — the hard and the much cheaper and slower floppy disk.

DNA fingerprinting a technology which identifies and codes a person's unique genetic make-up. Law-enforcement agencies around the world, including the FBI, are moving to establish a comprehensive DNA database. Employers and insurance companies are also anxious to use the technology in order to "screen out" people with undesirable genetic characteristics.

Electronic Funds Transfer at Point of Sale (EFTPOS) this technology makes possible multiple transactions using credit or debit facilities, usually with a card and PIN. Australia boasts the world's first genuine national EFTPOS system.

E-mail short for electronic mail sent by modem or through networks from user to user.

Encryption the process of translating a message into secret code.

Freedom of Information (FOI) legislation which allows people to view information held by government or other bodies. Access to personal information is an important element of privacy protection, even if its monetary cost is sometimes prohibitive.

Gateways machines that interconnect computer networks and translate between the different protocols of those networks. Also known as repeaters, bridges, packet routers and relays.

Generally available publication legal term for a document that contains information in the public domain (land records, company information, telephone numbers, and so on). In their raw form, these publications are exempt from the protection of privacy law.

Hacker it is believed that this word was coined by the founders of the Massachusetts Institute of Technology Artificial Intelligence lab to describe an expert computer user who obsessively explores the potential of computers or uses computers extensively as a form of recreation. In the early 1980s the term was picked up by law-enforcement officials, the media, and hackers themselves to describe those who break into computer systems, voice-mail systems and telephone systems. See also **cracker**.

Hardware the visible components of a computer, such as printers, **modems**, cables, et cetera.

Inferential statistics personal data which have been aggregated to represent the characteristics of a geographical unit or an element of the population. The Australian Bureau of Statistics releases such data on subdivisions of districts, and this allows direct marketers and others to calculate the likely profile, income, debt, occupation, family status and characterics of anyone living in a particular area.

Integrated Services Digital Network (ISDN) the framework of the emerging intelligent telephone network. By incorporating a "D" or data channel which carries non-voice information, the network is able to function with subscribers in an interactive manner.

Intellectual property a term used to refer to the intangible property arising from mental work. Patents, copyrights, trademarks and trade secrets are such examples. Software does not fit neatly into any of these categories, and how this property should be protected is under intense discussion in many countries.

Intelligent telephone network the newly emerging telephone system that provides a range of services such as **Call Return, Caller ID, Call Trace**, and so on. The intelligent network will also make possible interactive communications where a variety of transactions are possible over the telephone line.

Internet short for "Internetwork", a network of networks. Users on any computer on the internet can send **E-mail** and files can remotely log onto any other computer on the internet using one standard set of protocols. The internet is sometimes described as the global interlinkage of networks. See also **matrix**.

Kilobyte stands for 1024 bytes (2 to the tenth power is 1024). It is represented by the notation K.

Law Enforcement Access Network (LEAN) a massive information-matching project involving state and federal governments and utilising around 10,000 computer terminals.

Line blocking a facility which allows telephone callers to stop the transmission of their number to the receiving parties call display device. The blocking process applies to the entire number, and therefore to all calls originating from it with the exception of calls to emergency numbers and some audiotex numbers. Line blocking is sometimes invalid for toll-free numbers.

Lotus Marketplace a set of CD ROM disks offered by the Lotus development corporation in the US containing financial details relating to over a hundred million American families. A highly successful campaign by privacy advocates in 1991 forced the withdrawal of the product.

Magstripe a stripe on the back of a plastic card, such as a new Medicare card or credit card. The stripe carries a limited amount of basic information such as account number, name and expiry date.

Matrix a term coined by William Gibson in his book *Neuromancer* to refer to the world-wide network of computers.

Megabyte stands for 1,048,576 bytes (2 to the power of 20).

Microcomputer or **Micro** a computer that is small in size and capacity. Sometimes referred to as "personal computers" or "PCs".

Modem stands for modulator/demodulator, a device used to encode and decode binary codes into sounds in the voice frequency range of the telephone system. Allows for data transmission, including by fax, over voice lines.

Modified Electronic White Pages (MEWP) a computer program used by telecommunications carriers and law enforcement and tax agencies which gives a name from a given telephone number. A standard EWP provides name-to-number matching only.

Net or **Network** a set of computers using common protocols to communicate with each other. Five types of networks are research, company, cooperative, commercial, and "Metanetworks".

Networked community a set of people who use a network regularly to communicate with each other, and who without the network might not be able to function as a group.

Open Systems a system of computers and peripherals attached to network, all using common protocols for the functions. This compatibility is becoming more common, and will allow ready interchange and supply of hardware and software.

Opt In a term used for an exclusive system or list in which participation depends on the active consent or request of a person. Privacy advocates often argue that direct marketing should be on the basis of opt in, thus ensuring that unwanted advances are not made. In an opt-in system, direct marketers would compile lists on the basis of a person's voluntary request to be placed on a list.

Opt Out a term used for an inclusive system or list in which participation is automatic unless the person takes active steps to be removed from the system. The white pages telephone book is a common example of opt out.

Orwellism the fear or spectre of a **Big Brother** society. From George Orwell, the author of *1984*.

Password a string of characters known, or assumed to be known, only to one person. It is used by that computer operator to prove rights of entry to the system.

Personal or **Population Identification Number (PIN)** this term is used both in the sense of an access number to operate a computer or a general numbering system for a country or an administration. PINs are the backbone of the population-numbering systems found in many countries.

Photo-digitising a photographic process wherein photographic images can be stored electronically. The same technology makes photo-ageing possible.

Privacy the set of standards measuring the right of authorities, companies, institutions and persons to intrude into the affairs of establish surveillance over the individual. Sometimes confused with **Data protection**.

Privacy International (PI) the world network of privacy advocates and data protection experts.

Protocols specific standard algorithms that provide services on computers networks including **e-mail**, file transfer, remote log-in, and computer conferencing.

Psychological testing standard insurance procedure which attempts to generate sufficient information to compile a medical and psychological profile of an insurance candidate.

Phone phreak a person who breaks into telephone switching computers and makes free calls or alters calling options of subscribers.

Pragvocate short for "pragmatic advocate". A term coined originally by Simon Davies at the Computers, Freedom and Privacy Conference, San Francisco in 1991, as a pejorative term for advocates who corrode the process of reform by cutting deals in back-rooms instead of taking a strong public stand on an issue.

Public data network (PDN) any network that is open for general access. Contrasts with closed or private networks used by governments, industry groups or companies.

Random Access Memory (RAM) the high-speed computational memory of a computer. Random access means that the access time to any part of the stored data is the same. Disks, on the other hand, are not random because the data is stored in a particular location of the device.

Safe-T-Cam cute name for a dangerous scheme. Originally known as Scam Scan, this project of the New South Wales Government will install on public roads satellite-linked cameras which will read the number plates of vehicles and transmit information to a law-enforcement database.

Smart card a credit-card-sized personal computer. Sometimes known as a portable access control card. It may contain a chip microprocessor, or have a laser reading facility, allowing the storage of more than a **megabyte** of information. Smart cards are being pioneered in health care, government services and the finance industry.

Software an informal and generic term for computer programs, as opposed to computer **hardware**. Software is a set of instructions that a machine can directly or indirectly recognise and execute. Software, although stored on disks, has no physical form other than an electronic or magnetic form.

Stealth worm a complex computer virus with artificial intelligence and DNA-type replication and mutation ability. The stealth worm s able to penetrate sophisticated computer security systems.

Tax File Number (TFN) an administrative system in which taxpayers and government beneficiaries are allocated a unique number which is then used as the basis for record and information administration in the Tax Office. The number is also used as a basis for cross-referencing of files and information between departments.

Techno-terrorism term used for the wide variety of attacks upon computers, networks and installations. Techno-terrorism usually takes the form of malicious viruses and worms.

Tripartite Agencies the three areas of government most likely to invade rights and privacy: Law enforcement, government revenue, and social welfare.

Trojan horse a computer program which is advertised as performing an interesting or useful function, but when activated performs a different, and often damaging function.

Universal numbering system a development being explored by numerous telecommunications organisations around the world in which technology will be developed to give a person a life-long telephone number. The number would be active at every point on the globe and need never be changed. Motorola is developing the Iridium project which will see 77 networked satellites launched in pursuit of this aim.

Vehicle-tracking systems technology which uses "bugs" to monitor the movement and location of vehicles or even people. Lend Lease's Quicktrack system, developed in Australia, is one of the world's most highly advanced vehicle-tracking systems. Bugs can be activated from the central monitoring station and accuracy throughout the metropolitan area is accurate to within 30 metres.

Virus a computer program that makes a copy of itself inside an existing program. When the "host" program is started up, the virus is activated, and takes over.

Voice mail an extension of **e-mail** in which the human voice can be translated into binary code and stored in computer files and played back later.

Workplace surveillance usually involves the use of special software programs designed to monitor the work patterns and productivity of employees. Can also involve the use of more conventional surveillance techniques such as closed-circuit television.

Worm a computer program that makes copies of itself within a computer or between computers in a network. Has similar characteristics to the **Trojan horse**.

LIST OF ACRONYMS
AND ABBREVIATIONS

AAT	Administrative Appeals Tribunal
ABA	Australian Bankers' Association
ABC	Australian Broadcasting Corporation
ABCI	Australian Bureau of Criminal Intelligence
ABS	Australian Bureau of Statistics
ACS	Australian Customs Service
ADF	Australian Doctors' Fund
AEO	Australian Electoral Office
AFP	Australian Federal Police
A-G's	Attorney-General's Department
AHACSS	Australian Health and Aged Care Systems Seminar
ALP	Australian Labor Party
ALRC	Australian Law Reform Commission
AMA	Australian Medical Association
APF	Australian Privacy Foundation
ASIO	Australian Security Intelligence Organisation
AT&T	American Telephone and Telegraph Company
ATM	Automatic Teller Machine
ATO	Australian Tax Office
BD&M	Births Deaths and Marriages
CCL	Council for Civil Liberties
CD ROM	Compact Disk Read Only Memory
CHIPS	Clearing House for Interbank Payment Systems (US)
CIA	Central Intelligence Agency (US)
CLI	Calling Line Identification
CPSR	Computer Professionals for Social Responsibility (US)
CRAA	Credit Reference Association of Australia
CSRCCE	Commission for the Safety, Rehabilitation and Compensation of Commonwealth Employees
CTRA	Cash Transactions Reporting Agency
DAS	Department of Administrative Services

DEET	Department of Employment, Education and Training
DILGEA	Department of Immigration, Local Government and Ethnic Affairs
DIR	Department of Industrial Relations
DPP	Director of Public Prosecutions
DSD	Defence Signals Directorate
DSS	Department of Social Security
DVA	Department of Veterans' Affairs
EC	European Commission
EFT	Electronic Funds Transfer
EFTPOS	Electronic Funds Transfer at Point of Sale
FOI	Freedom of Information
HCN	Health Communications Network
HIC	Health Insurance Commission
HREOC	Human Rights and Equal Opportunity Commission
ICAC	Independent Commission Against Corruption (NSW)
ID	Identity (card)
IPPs	Information Privacy Principles
IRS	Internal Revenue Service (US)
ISDN	Integrated Services Digital Network
IT	Information Technology
LEAN	Law Enforcement Access Network
MDC	Medical Data Card
MP	Member of Parliament
NCA	National Crime Authority
NCCL	New South Wales Council for Civil Liberties
NSA	National Security Agency (US)
OECD	Organisation for Economic Cooperation and Developme
OMB	Office of Management and Business (US)
PBS	Pharmaceutical Benefits Scheme
PC	Personal Computer
PI	Privacy Internationl
PIN	Personal Identification Number or Population Identification Number
RTA	Roads and Traffic Authority (NSW)
SMH	*Sydney Morning Herald*
TFN	Tax File Number
VCCL	Victorian Council for Civil Liberties

APPENDIX OF DIAGRAMS

ZONES OF SURVEILLANCE

Australia has progessed from the upper part
of Zone 2 in the early 1970s to the lower
part of Zone 4 in the 1990s.

ZONE 5
**TOTAL
SURVEILLANCE**

ZONE 4
**MASS
SURVEILLANCE**

ZONE 3
**ROUTINE
SURVEILLANCE**

ZONE 2
**CONDITIONAL
SURVEILLANCE**

ZONE 1
**RESTRICTED
SURVEILLANCE**

AUSTRALIA AS A SURVEILLANCE SOCIETY

The estimated extent of surveillance of the Australian community from 1972 to 1997 (projected).

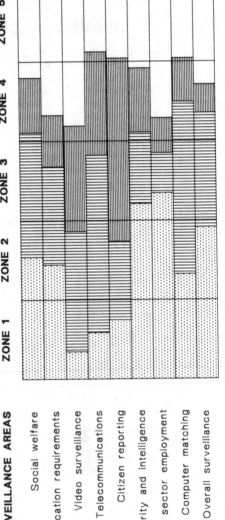

SURVEILLANCE AREAS

Social welfare

Identification requirements

Video surveillance

Telecommunications

Citizen reporting

National security and intelligence

Public sector employment

Computer matching

Overall surveillance

ZONE 1   ZONE 2   ZONE 3   ZONE 4   ZONE 5

1972

1992

1997 (projected)

SURVEILLANCE THROUGH COMPUTER LINKING

Estimates of the increase in Australia's database linkage from 1972 to 1997 (projected).

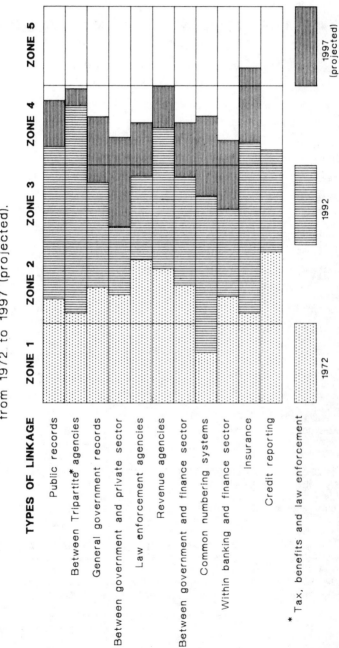

TYPES OF LINKAGE

- Public records
- Between Tripartite* agencies
- General government records
- Between government and private sector
- Law enforcement agencies
- Revenue agencies
- Between government and finance sector
- Common numbering systems
- Within banking and finance sector
- Insurance
- Credit reporting

ZONE 1   ZONE 2   ZONE 3   ZONE 4   ZONE 5

1972   1992   1997 (projected)

* Tax, benefits and law enforcement

THE INTERNATIONAL INTELLIGENCE NETWORK

The Quadrapartite Agreement

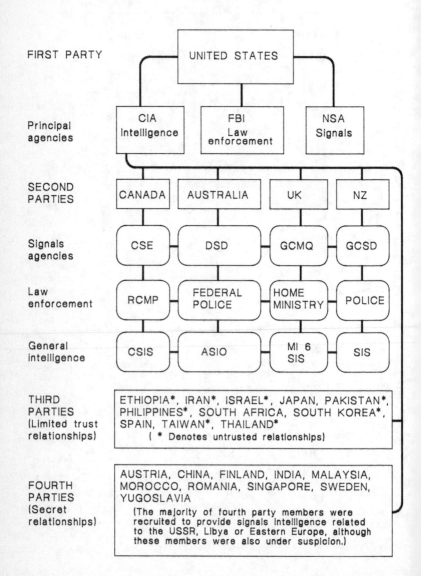

FIRST PARTY	UNITED STATES		
Principal agencies	CIA Intelligence	FBI Law enforcement	NSA Signals
SECOND PARTIES	CANADA	AUSTRALIA	UK	NZ
Signals agencies	CSE	DSD	GCMQ	GCSD
Law enforcement	RCMP	FEDERAL POLICE	HOME MINISTRY	POLICE
General intelligence	CSIS	ASIO	MI 6 SIS	SIS

THIRD PARTIES (Limited trust relationships)

ETHIOPIA*, IRAN*, ISRAEL*, JAPAN, PAKISTAN*, PHILIPPINES*, SOUTH AFRICA, SOUTH KOREA*, SPAIN, TAIWAN*, THAILAND*
(* Denotes untrusted relationships)

FOURTH PARTIES (Secret relationships)

AUSTRIA, CHINA, FINLAND, INDIA, MALAYSIA, MOROCCO, ROMANIA, SINGAPORE, SWEDEN, YUGOSLAVIA

(The majority of fourth party members were recruited to provide signals intelligence related to the USSR, Libya or Eastern Europe, although these members were also under suspicion.)

THE CIRCULATION OF PERSONAL INFORMATION

SOME MAIN INFORMATION FLOWS TO AND FROM THE COMMONWEALTH GOVERNMENT
(NOT INCLUDING LINKAGE WITHIN PRIVATE SECTOR, STATE GOVERNMENT, OR LAW ENFORCEMENT)

WHAT YOUR TELEPHONE NUMBER CAN REVEAL ABOUT YOU

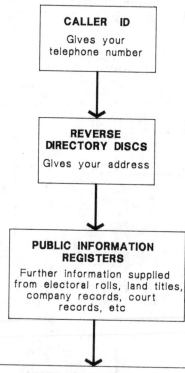

CALLER ID

Gives your
telephone number

↓

**REVERSE
DIRECTORY DISCS**

Gives your address

↓

**PUBLIC INFORMATION
REGISTERS**

Further information supplied
from electoral rolls, land titles,
company records, court
records, etc

↓

STATISTICAL DATA

(Inferential data based on the census, and
drawn from aggregated information from each
suburban block in Australia.)

Marital status, age, religion, aboriginality, birthplace,
labour force status, proficiency in English, type of
relationship in household, family income, single parent
information, type of dwelling, school leaving age, level
and field of qualification, income, occupation, household
type for the unemployed, monthly mortgage payments,
weekly rent, number of vehicles, method of travel to
work, nature of occupancy, etc.

USEFUL ADDRESSES

The Australian Privacy Charter Council
School of Law
University of New South Wales
PO Box 1
Kensington NSW 2033

(Public support and offers of assistance are greatly appreciated.)

The Australian Privacy Foundation
PO Box R507
Royal Exchange
Sydney NSW 2000

(Membership of the foundation is $30 per year.)

The Privacy Commissioner
Human Rights and Equal Opportunity Commission
Level 24
American Express Building
388 George Street
Sydney NSW 2000

(The Privacy Commissioner also offers a toll-free number for questions or complaints on 008 023 985.)

The Privacy Committee of New South Wales
GPO Box 6
Sydney NSW 2001
Telephone: (02) 252 3843

(The Privacy Committee is able to investigate and conciliate any matter relating to an aspect of privacy invasion or suveillance in New South Wales.)

The Privacy Committee of South Australia
13th Floor
SGIC Building
Victoria Square
Adelaide SA 5000

(The Privacy Committee is able to investigate and conciliate any matter relating to an aspect of privacy invasion or surveillance in South Australia.)

Privacy International
CPSR
Suite 303
666 Pennsylvania Avenue SE
Washington DC 20003
United States of America

Credit Reference Association of Australia
Public Access Division
PO Box 964
North Sydney NSW 2059

(You will need to provide in your letter your full name; current residential address; previous address, if you have lived at your current address less than three years; date of birth; and driver's licence number. The CRAA does not accept postal addresses. One of the important benefits to the credit industry of consumer access to files is that it also allows the CRAA to update its information on you. Post boxes would not be much use.)

ACKNOWLEDGEMENTS

I would like to take this opportunity to offer my appreciation to some supportive friends and colleagues who have made this book possible.

My thanks go first to my privacy mentors, Graham Greenleaf, Marc Rotenberg, Roger Clarke, David Flaherty and Michael Kirby. To Bill Reddin and Peter Garrett for generous support and advice when I needed it most. To Tim Dixon for (unwittingly) getting me started in privacy and for being such an unfaltering friend. To Brian Wilshire, who demonstrated the importance of rocking the boat. To Julie Cameron and Maureen Tangney whose judgement and integrity is without peer. To my father, for being my greatest supporter.

Ian Black gave crucial support and advice, for which I am extremely grateful.

I must also thank a large number of people who have contributed in one way or another to the creation of this book. They include Andrei Roszczynski, Wayne Madsen, Pierrot Peladeau, Julianne Wargren, Neil Watkinson, Brendan Palmer, Joe Bryant, Peter Catts, Jim Rule, Ron Castan, Stephen Watson, David White, Bob Eggins, Janine Haines, Glen Krawczek, Jim Nolan, Barry Wilson, Nadia Weiner, Leon Jones, David Burnham, Linda Werbeloff, Paul Zannetti, Jacqueline Morgan, Bruce Shepherd, Nigel Waters, Michael Walters, John Wallace, the late Ben Lexcen, and especially to my dear friend Peter.

I would also like to express my gratitude to the staff of the Australian Privacy Commissioner, the NSW Privacy Committee, the Australian Bureau of Statistics, Computer Professionals for Social Responsibility (Washington DC), the State Library of New South Wales, the Australian Doctors' Fund, to Senators Kay Patterson, Bronwyn Bishop, Ron Boswell and their staff, and to the many members of the Australian Privacy Foundation and Privacy International who provided information and advice. Thanks also to Jay Thorwaldson and Peter Denning for some of the Glossary definitions.

The Faculty of Law of the University of New South Wales took me under its' wing at a crucial time and this good faith was of inestimable importance to me.

INDEX